# MIRACLE
## ON DEATH ROW

Judge Kermit C. Bradford

Published by

chosen books
Distributed by Word Books. Publisher • Waco. Texas 76703

Scripture quotations are from the King James Version of the Bible.

For the protection of those concerned, a few of the names—but none of the facts—have been changed in this book.

ISBN 0-912376-17-1

With all the love that I can know, I dedicate this book to my wonderful mama:

Fannie Mae Bradford

Who, through love, devotion, sacrifice and faithfulness to her God, brought to my heart the precious message of the Gospel—Jesus Christ.

She faithfully ministered to all who passed her way, meeting the needs of the lost, suffering, sick humanity through labor, sacrifice and love.

My heart shall ever be grateful for her life, and my life shall forever be indebted to her for having pointed me toward "the way, the truth, and the life."

K. C. B.

# Contents

# Acknowledgments

I wish to express my appreciation to my patient, loving wife, Thelma, who provided steady encouragement through the years of writing and rewriting that went into this manuscript. Her continual prayers and wise counsel helped give me comfort and direction.

I want to thank my administrative secretary, Freda R. Turner, who has spent many hours, day and night, typing the manuscript, proofreading, and selflessly giving herself to meet publishing deadlines.

I desire to express my gratitude to Martha Quick Denny who read and analyzed my manuscript, and offered suggestions for revision and technical advice; and finally, but really foremost, Mr. Maynard Marsh, who encouraged me to undertake this project and whose faith and counsel stood me in good stead from first to last.

# Foreword

While attending a convention back in the middle sixties, I heard a dynamic criminal defense lawyer tell a story that electrified the audience. The people sensed through the light in his eyes and the fire in his being that here was a man who knew Jesus. It was about a murder case he defended which had a series of bizarre turnings, climaxed by a miracle of God.

Fascinated by both the man and his story, I met Kermit Bradford after the program. "That's the most exciting story I've ever heard," I said to him. "You should write a book."

Years passed, and Lawyer Bradford had become a judge. The next time our paths crossed I asked, "How is the book coming?" He smiled, "I'm working on it."

*Miracle on Death Row* not only gives us a behind-the-scenes look at one of America's most unusual murder trials, it shows us how a loving God can penetrate the minds and hearts of His rebellious, resistant children.

Thrust into the world on his own at the age of twelve after the death of his father, Kermit Bradford spent his early years in pursuit of high adventure and excitement through boxing, stunt flying, and as a U.S. military intelligence agent with the British intelligence in London and the French Underground in Paris during World War II. He even had a fling at Hollywood acting. Finally, he chose law as his profession and began a colorful, action-packed career as a trial lawyer.

Lawyer Bradford met the greatest challenge of his life when he represented Tommy Callahan, a young man charged with murder. He believed that every defendant deserves a fair trial, no matter how shocking the indictment.

This case not only demanded the utmost effort and skill but tested Kermit Bradford to the limit of his legal talents, forcing him to meet and overcome a series of unbelievable obstacles. It was also a case that miraculously turned around the lives of two men, one facing bitter defeat, the other facing death in the electric chair.

When you have read the last chapter of this incredible story you will feel that you have been carried far beyond the confines of a courtroom and plunged into great depths of human emotions—from hate and murder to love and sacrifice.

It is not often you find a book that has an absorbing dramatic story and at the same time honors Jesus Christ. *Miracle on Death Row* is such a book.

MAYNARD R. MARSH
Field Representative
Billy Graham Evangelistic Association

# 1

## The Murder

It was quiet in downtown Atlanta that sultry July evening. By 10:00 P.M. most of the houses and shops on dingy Trinity Avenue were already dark. At Kilman's all-night grocery store, fifty-nine-year-old R. E. Kilman started checking the supplies on his shelves. He'd returned just that afternoon from a vacation and stock was low.

At 10:20 P.M. his good-looking red-headed son, Howard, age thirty, waited on two customers, rang up the sales and, expecting little further business, sat down behind the front counter to tally up the day's receipts. At the top of the column he wrote: July 6, 1951.

In the back of the store, R. E. Kilman opened the frozen meat chest. As the slender gray-haired man pulled out pad and pencil he imagined he could still hear the sound of ocean waves off Virginia Beach, taste the tang of raw clams and fresh boiled lobster. He glanced toward Howard and felt a surge of gratitude for his hard-working son. How fortunate he was to have him safely back home from the Korean War to help out in the store so that he himself could begin to take a little trip now and then.

Kilman was bent over the chest, counting packaged meat, when two masked men entered the store. So absorbed was he in his inventory that he did not look up at the sound of voices. Only when his son shouted, "Look out, Dad!" did he straighten up.

Even then it took a few seconds for his mind to register what his eyes saw. Two men wearing sunglasses, with handkerchiefs hiding the lower part of their faces, were standing at the front counter. The taller one, who wore a white handkerchief, carried a sawed-off shotgun. The other one, in a black mask, held a pistol.

The grocer saw Howard grab for the revolver the Kilmans had recently started keeping under the counter. In the same instant orange flame spurted from the pistol in the shorter man's hand. Three shots exploded in the quiet store. The bullets slammed into young Kilman's chest and neck. He was jolted backward by the impact of the slugs, like a puppet yanked by a string, and fell against a chair.

"My God!" Kilman shouted. "You've shot my son!"

He lunged under the rear counter, where the Kilmans kept a second pistol, and began firing wildly at his son's assailant.

Bullets ricocheted through the store. One tore through a box of cornflakes, another into a sack of potatoes, a third ripped open a can of soup. The man with the shotgun seemed paralyzed with indecision. Then he bolted for the door, shouting something that sounded like, "Let's get out of here, Claude!" The black-masked gunman backed out behind him, firing at the father.

Kilman raced after the retreating men, disregarding the bullets screaming past him. Outside he saw one gunman slamming the front door of an automobile, the other scrambling into the rear seat. The dark gray sedan shot forward, sideswiping a parked car, and then roared down the street with the grocer emptying his pistol at it. His face was contorted with frustration and grief as he shook the empty pistol in his fist at them, screaming, "No, no, no—you can't come into my store and shoot my son and get away with it—you'll answer to God for this night's work."

Kilman then ran back into the store to his son. Howard was slumped on his stool, his hand still clenching the unused revolver. Blood spurted from his neck and chest. Even as his father held him, Howard sagged to the floor, the gun slipping from his fingers. Cradling his son in his lap, Kilman begged, "Oh, God, don't let my boy die."

In a few minutes a squad car arrived, summoned by neighbors. The officer radioed for an ambulance, and soon, siren wailing, red light flashing, the Grady Hospital rescue unit pulled up. A medic in white dashed through the cluster of people outside the grocery store and examined young Kilman for signs of life. Two .22

caliber bullets were lodged in his chest, one in his neck. Turning to the older grocer, the medic shook his head. "He's dead."

Saturday morning, July 7, began like any other weekend in our homey three-bedroom ranch-style house, across town from the scene of the murder.

My petite wife, Thelma, was in the kitchen preparing breakfast. I watched her as she moved about. She had on a pink apron and her raven black hair was up in pin curls. I thought to myself, she is just as cute in the morning as she is in an evening gown.

I settled our beautiful brown-eyed three-year-old daughter, Brenda, in her high chair. With Brenda contentedly sloshing orange juice on her bib, I opened the *Atlanta Constitution.*

BANDITS SHOOT GROCER TO DEATH, the large headline read. FATHER ESCAPES IN BLAZING BATTLE.

An Atlanta grocer was killed late Friday and his father narrowly escaped death or injury in a pistol battle with two masked bandits at their store. Howard N. Kilman, 30, was shot at the cash register as he reached for a pistol when the gunmen entered. His father, R. E. Kilman, 59, who was in the rear of the store, grabbed his pistol and fired at the bandits. Witnesses said the bandits  both white men—ran from the store and leaped into a getaway car waiting near the intersection of Trinity Avenue and Memorial Drive. A third man waited in the car, described as an old-model, slate-colored sedan.

Thelma came into the breakfast nook, her delicately pretty face flushed from cooking and her deep-set blue eyes sparkling. "Mr. Bradford," she said sweetly, "since today is Saturday, I have prepared your favorite breakfast: banana pancakes, sausage and black coffee."

"You're all I want," I said, pulling her down on my lap and giving her a resounding kiss and savoring the aroma of fresh bananas. Thelma scanned the newspaper article. "How awful!" she said. "That poor father; I hope they catch those men fast."

"I hope they do, too, honey," I said. "And I hope they give them the same they gave that young grocer."

Finishing breakfast and picking up my briefcase, I reached over and kissed little Brenda good-bye, wiping her syrup off my chin.

"I wish I could stay home today, but I have paperwork to do at the office on the embezzlement case I am defending on Monday. Winning this one is important to me."

Thelma became very serious. "Winning is always important to you, Brad. Perhaps too much so. Don't you think it's possible to learn quite a bit from a defeat?"

I thought about that for a moment, then reached for her hand. "I don't think winning is everything," I replied. "I think trying to win is what counts. But you're good for me, dear." We walked to the door together.

On the way to the office I dropped by my mother's house. Thelma was concerned again about her appar-

ent failing health from the asthma that had plagued
her for years. Parking the car in her driveway, I
climbed the steps to her small white frame dwelling
and walked in without ringing the doorbell. I heard
voices in the front room. There was my mother, on her
knees, her arm around the shoulder of a neighbor,
obviously praying for her needs.

As I waited quietly in the hallway for them to con-
clude the prayer, that little scene brought back my
boyhood! Here was my mama as I remembered her,
giving help and comfort to others. One of my earliest
memories was of the worldwide influenza epidemic in
1917–18 which claimed about 500,000 lives in the
United States. I was about eight years old and we
were living in the city of Atlanta when I came home
from play one day to see policemen cordoning off a
block near us with ropes and signs: WARNING. CON-
TAGIOUS AREA. INFLUENZA. DO NOT ENTER.

I had run home to tell Mama and found her packing
a small black bag with soap, toothbrush, bottles of various medicines, and her Bible. She said, "Son, I've got
to go help." She let me walk with her as far as the
corner where the rope had been stretched. There she
bent down and kissed me good-bye.

"They said people in the next few blocks are dying
like flies," she whispered sorrowfully. "There are so
few nurses, I must do what I can to help the sick and
dying. I won't be allowed home until the epidemic is
over. Aunt Nancy will care for you until I return."

"But—but what if you catch it, too?" I asked fear-
fully.

"The good Lord will take care of me," she answered confidently.

My mother, Fannie Mae Bradford, tall and erect, with flaming red hair and the zeal of a missionary, walked away into that deadly contagious neighborhood.

And, I reflected now, God had protected her. And here, many years later, she was still ministering to a neighbor in need. I waited restlessly until she completed her mission and the neighbor had left.

Mama then filled me in on her health and her week's doings. "We have a new preacher in our church, Kermit," she added, "and I want you and Thelma to meet him. He is such a powerful man of God."

I nodded absently; Mama was always trying to get me interested in church. Back in the car, later, I smiled sadly to myself over her continuous efforts to get people to surrender their lives to Jesus Christ, particularly her son. For some people—like Mama and Thelma—this kind of thing was fine, but not for me. I wasn't an atheist; I believed in a Higher Power; it was just that I didn't have time to waste going to church.

I was on my way up. After serving four years in the Army Counter Intelligence Corps in World War II, I had started to practice law on my own in Atlanta. Now, six years later, I was doing well. The way to get ahead was to work harder and study harder than anyone else and to battle tenaciously for every advantage. If you

didn't, there were ten other guys waiting for your rung
on the ladder. I was too busy to think seriously about
my spiritual life.

The Kilman murder was front-page news for days.
Since I knew many of the detectives assigned to the
case, I followed the press accounts with more than
casual interest. The first real break came the second
day. A man named Roberson had noticed a strange car
parked in front of his house and called the police.
Homicide detectives quickly arrived on the scene and
analyzed every inch of the automobile. Several .22
caliber cartridges were scattered about the back seat;
a set of fingerprints was discovered that belonged to a
man named Billy Joe Tinch, a convict on parole.

On Wednesday newspapers broke the story of the
arrest of a suspect, Clyde Tinch, a twenty-five-year-
old minister. Clyde had signed a statement linking his
brother, Billy Joe Tinch, and a friend, T. C. Callahan,
with the murder of the grocer. Both Billy Joe Tinch
and T. C. Callahan were still at large.

After supper Wednesday evening the three of us
settled down in the den and Thelma picked up the
evening *Journal*. "I can't believe this, Brad," she said.
"That young man arrested in connection with the
murder is a minister! The paper says he's been an
evangelist holding revivals since the age of fourteen."

"It's a strange twist," I agreed.

"I think it's terrible," my wife continued. "A

preacher involved in a murder! I wonder what your mother must think of this."

"It'll come as a shock," I said. "But face it, honey, this is one of the things wrong with the world today, we don't know who to honor, who to trust and who to follow," I said in disgust.

At that moment Brenda climbed onto my lap with a tattered copy of *Scat! Scat! Striped Cat*, the current bedtime favorite.

Half an hour later I lifted a protesting little girl to my shoulders and carried her to the bedroom Thelma had decorated so lovingly in pastel greens and pinks. Over the small white French Provincial bed was a picture of Jesus holding a lamb.

Brenda prolonged the undressing process as long as she could. Finally, she knelt beside her bed and with bowed head and folded hands began to pray, "Now I lay me down to sleep . . . ." The "God blesses" took a while, but at last she jumped up, gave me a hug, and bounced into bed.

I left her room with the glow I always felt when I heard her pray, unaware that something important was lacking in my life. It would be brought home shockingly to me, later, that while we had taught Brenda to pray—I really didn't know how to pray myself.

On Friday, the thirteenth of July, the papers reported that Clyde Tinch had testified before the Fulton County Grand Jury. As a result of the hearing, the

grand jury had returned murder indictments against
T. C. Callahan, Billy Joe Tinch, and two others sus-
pected as being accomplices in the July 6 slaying of
Howard Kilman.

On the same day federal warrants were issued by
the U.S. Commissioner in Atlanta charging T. C. Callahan and Billy Joe Tinch with unlawful flight to avoid
prosecution. The FBI joined in the manhunt.

Three weeks passed. Then on August 2, headlines
in the *Atlanta Constitution* proclaimed: SLAYING
SUSPECT CAUGHT BY FBI IN PHILADELPHIA.

> Atlanta officers Thursday completed legal steps to
> return to Georgia, Thomas C. Callahan, 25-year-old
> paroled convict arrested in Philadelphia, Pa., as
> Federal officers pushed a search for Callahan's
> accomplice who was indicted with Callahan for the
> holdup slaying of a grocer here.

The article went on to list a long record of law viola-
tions by Callahan. A common criminal, I concluded,
throwing the paper aside in disgust.

# 2

## The Defense Lawyer

Three months passed; the Kilman murder case was relegated to the back pages of the papers, and then—except for a brief announcement that Billy Joe Tinch had been apprehended in Ohio and returned to Georgia—disappeared altogether, to make way for new tragedies, new sensations.

On October 30, 1951, I was in my law office when my legal secretary, Mrs. Elliott Lawton, buzzed me on the intercom: "Judge George Whitman is on the line." The judge was a distinguished, much-admired leader in the community.

"Good morning, Judge," I said into the telephone. "It's good to hear your voice—what can I do for you?"

"Mr. Bradford, I'm calling to ask a favor for the court." Judge Whitman went on to say that weeks ago at an arraignment in court he had appointed an attorney to represent an indigent defendant indicted for murder. After a preliminary investigation the attorney selected asked to be released from the case. "Mr.

Bradford, I've called to ask if you will accept an appointment to represent the defendant?"

I knew these court-appointed defense cases. They were often frustrating and time-consuming. Yet our legal code of ethics says in part that a lawyer is bound to undertake the defense of a person accused of a crime regardless of his personal opinion as to the guilt of the accused. I replied, "I'll be happy to help out, who is the defendant?"

"It's *The State versus T. C. Callahan,*" answered the judge. "Thank you, Mr. Bradford, you can pick up a copy of the indictment in the Clerk's Office."

I sat for a moment staring at the receiver in my hand. Then I buzzed Mrs. Lawton. "T. C. Callahan! Isn't he—wasn't he connected with that grocery-store murder over on Trinity Avenue a while back that made the headlines for a month or so?"

Mrs. Lawton thought he was. From what I recalled from newspaper accounts it had been a particularly violent affair. One court-appointed lawyer had already turned back the case. It must be an electric-chair case.

I was glumly reviewing these prospects when Mrs. Lawton came in from the outer office and sat down across the desk from me. She was not only a skillful and efficient secretary, but a refined Christian lady with a gentleness about her that bespoke of her loving concern for other people.

"It is strange that the judge should call me; I'm not on the court-appointed list," I began.

"Mr. Bradford, I have a very peculiar feeling that

God is in this case somehow, and that the Lord wants to do a work in your life and in the life of the accused young man," she said.

"That is a sobering thought, Mrs. Lawton, and I do appreciate your concern." When she returned to her desk I thought to myself that she was a lot like my mother. Strange are these women who love God; they seem to have it all figured out. I wish I did!

When she was gone I swung my big leather chair to the window and looked out at the city skyline— isolated from the noises of the street thirteen stories below. As always, mention of God brought my child- hood rushing back. My mind returned now to the dark- est days of my life. I was twelve years old when I was called into my father, Leonard Bradford's, sickroom. Papa's usually deep voice sounded strangely thin as he said, "Son, the doctor says I have tuberculosis and must go away to the sanatorium. I hate to tell you this, but you cannot go back to school in the fall. You will have to get a job and help out here at home."

With those few words all of my dreams for the future seemed to be wiped out. "Please, Papa," I begged, "I don't mind working to help Mama, but let me stay in school. You always told me the best way to help the family was to get an education."

My heart was throbbing as I awaited his answer. "But you can't work and go to school at the same time," he said.

"I could work in the afternoon and at night until I finish high school, then get a regular job."

Papa stirred on his pillows, studying my face for a moment. "All right, son," he said, his voice broken by his labored breathing. "If you think you can do both, go ahead. I am sorry it has to be this way."

My father, before his illness, was a good-looking, ambitious, strong-willed, strong-bodied farmer. He had hoped that by leaving the farm and coming to the big city in the early 1900's he could get into the growing automobile industry. He was one of the first car mechanics in Atlanta and had his own automobile repair business, and was starting to make good money when he was stricken with TB.

As I turned to leave the room, I looked at Mama; her face was wet with silent tears and her deep, sympathizing compassion for me was etched in every line of her face. I wanted to run to her and feel her strong, comforting arms about me. But I couldn't, it was too late! It was time to grow up.

It was Mama's strength and love at that moment that kept me from despair. I hurried out so that she wouldn't see my tears.

My twelve-year-old world quickly changed. By summer's end I was working at the corner drugstore, clerking at a grocery, mowing lawns and delivering newspapers. After Papa's death, I continued this routine until I finished high school. My first full-time job was as office boy with the Western Union Telegraph Company, where I worked myself up to clerk and then bookkeeper, going to accounting school at night.

By this time I had become accepted by the fast-moving group of people in our department who ran things. When they invited me to one of their weekend parties at Mountain Park, Georgia, back in the early thirties, I felt I really had arrived.

About ten couples of us drove up on a Saturday afternoon to a large rustic cabin deep in the woods, near a beautiful lake. The girls unloaded the food from the cars and began to cook up a lavish meal. One of the executives opened a gallon of corn whiskey and began to pour drinks. When I took my first gulp, it burned my throat going down and set my stomach on fire. Soon my head began to spin, then someone handed me another drink and another. Dimly, I was aware of the others laughing, eating, drinking, dancing to the music of a phonograph. My date and I seemed to be caught up in the flow of the party. After a while some of the couples slipped out to their parked cars. Others drifted casually into the various bedrooms for the night, and a few had a rendezvous down at the lake for a nude bathing party.

The next morning I had a mammoth hangover and a worried conscience. But at breakfast all of the regulars, including the girls, patted me on the back and said how well I had handled myself the night before. I really was accepted now.

During the months that followed I reminded myself that I had never had much time for fun as a boy. I had a right now to "sow a few wild oats." Striving for success in the business world, hungry for recognition and popularity, I decided that the outdated values of my boyhood were simply irrelevant to the fuller life I was enjoying.

Several years passed, during which my quest for excitement took me into stunt flying, Golden Gloves boxing, and acting with the Theater Guild. One Saturday night some friends and I had a table at Moonlight Gardens, a large, beautiful dance hall across the street from the Fox Theater on Peachtree Street. As the dance band began to play, the spotlight picked up a petite fresh-faced young girl behind the microphone. She had deep blue eyes and shoulder-length curly black hair. Her curvaceous figure was set off by a form-fitting black satin gown. Her voice was surprisingly rich and vibrant. She was singing, "Dinah—is there anyone finer . . . ."

I walked up to the bandstand to get a closer look. She was faintly familiar—then I remembered—I had met her at a dinner party the year before. Her name was Thelma Kirby. I asked her for a dance, reminding her of our previous introduction.

I held her closely as we danced and knew that I had something very special in my arms. We began seeing each other regularly. She was a wholesome, warm-hearted girl and I enjoyed her company. One night it would be the theater, then dinner and an occasional Saturday night dance with friends.

Our friendship began to turn into something more

personal. One night, in high spirits, after a couple of drinks I impetuously became very amorous. She pulled away quickly.

In my crowd heavy petting was so standard that I had assumed all girls wanted it this way.

"What's the matter?" I asked in bewilderment. "Don't you like me?"

"I care for you very much," she replied, "but I do not want our relationship to become—well, so physical. I'm sorry."

Then she told me about her rather sheltered childhood and the years at a church-oriented girls' school. She had learned to sing in church choirs. Out of it all had come strong convictions about dating and living a life which would be pleasing to God.

To my surprise, this gentle but firm rejection attracted me more than ever. Thelma had an elusive quality that none of the other girls I had ever dated possessed. Perhaps, in spite of the black satin, it was her innocence, her tremendous zest for life. Though I considered her faith naive, I was glad she had it for her sake. When she questioned me about my beliefs, I told her I believed in God and went to church. In this respect I was not as honest with her as she was with me.

Three years after we met we were married at the Wesley Memorial Methodist Church, and now I really had a reason to work hard. I attended a night accounting school and received my degree. Within the next few years I was promoted to accountant, statistician, auditor.

After thirteen years in accounting it was not much of a challenge to me anymore. I decided to look around for something a little more exciting, something not involving ledgers and figures, but a more people-centered career. Challenged by the thought of delving into the law and championing a cause in court, I enrolled in a night law college. In due time I'd received my Bachelor's and Master's degrees, passed the State Bar examination and hung out my shingle to practice law. I'd come a long way, I reflected, from the boy who had nearly left school at twelve.

With a start I returned from my memories to the present. "Mrs. Lawton, please make up a file folder on Callahan. I'll be going to the Fulton Tower Jail to see him this afternoon. The charge is robbery and murder. You can put a red tab on the folder. I feel that the prosecutor is going after the death penalty in this case."

3

# The Defendant

In the shadow of the Georgia State Capitol stands Fulton Tower, a dreary gray stone prison with medieval-looking turrets. On the way there to talk to Callahan I stopped at the Fulton County Courthouse to see Frank French, the solicitor general, who would be heading up the prosecution. French was in his mid-forties, tough-minded, hard-driving. There was an amused glint in his eyes as he greeted me.

"Bradford, you really have a loser this time," he began.

It was probably useless to attempt plea bargaining, yet I had to make the effort. "I haven't discussed the case with Callahan, but before I do I need to know whether the State would consider a guilty plea."

French leaned back in his chair, put his feet on the desk and laughed. "Not a chance, Bradford. We got your boy cold. He's gonna burn."

"Not without a fight, he's not," I snapped. But as I left his office, I admitted to myself that French was in

38

a strong position. Arrayed against me and the accused
were the solicitor general, his large and capable staff
of assistants and investigators, the scientific facilities
of the county crime laboratory, and the Atlanta Police
Department Detective Bureau. Callahan's only re-
source was one very hardheaded, stubborn lawyer
who hated to lose a case. I would defend his rights, as
the law demanded, but the odds against him were
very high.

I left my car in the Fulton Prison parking lot, and
pushed the buzzer beside the heavy iron gate. One of
the jailers peered out and recognized me. With a
clanking of heavy bolts, the iron door swung open.

As the jailer wrote out my pass he said, "They say
this fellow Callahan is dangerous—he's supposed to
be the triggerman in that murder. I'll be glad to send a
couple of guards with you upstairs."

With some disdain, I shook off the suggestion. As a
former boxer, along with my tough FBI training in
World War II, I considered myself physically able to
take care of what might come up.

The elevator carried me up to the maximum security floor where the jailer on duty escorted me down
the corridor to Callahan's cell. He unlocked the cell
door, saying, "Lawyer Bradford is here to see you."

I stepped in and the jailer locked the door behind
me. "Just holler out when you're ready to leave."

The young man accused of murder was sitting on
his bunk with his back to me. He wore the white and
tan prison uniform, and as he stood up I was surprised

to see how short he was—not more than five foot five. But, though small, he was powerfully built, with a supple, narrow waist; his gray-blue eyes were assessing me coolly. I concluded—yes, he could be very dangerous.

"I'm a lawyer," I said, "and the court has appointed me to defend you at your trial. My name is Bradford." I reached over to shake hands. His hand was ice-cold.

"Where is the other guy—I mean the other lawyer the court appointed?" he asked suspiciously.

"I haven't talked to him, but he decided not to represent you. I guess he felt that he couldn't win your case."

"Oh," the accused replied without expression.

"Now, sit down, Callahan. I'll need a lot of information from you."

"Mr. Bradford, I want you to know that I did not kill that man."

Of course not, I thought wearily. These young criminals are always innocent as newborn babes. "Don't give me a snow job," I said. "Whether you killed young Kilman or not, you'll get a fair trail and I'll defend you to the best of my ability."

"I didn't kill him," he muttered stonily.

"Perhaps not," I said, opening my briefcase and pulling out some papers. But I have your three-page criminal record here and it's not pretty. You've been in trouble since your teens."

Callahan tensed. "Where did you get that?"

"The same place the prosecution got it. And while

they can't introduce your past record at the trial, you can be sure it will be on their minds. The only way we'll make any headway, Callahan, is if you're absolutely honest with me. If you lie to me, we're both going to look bad in the courtroom."

I sat down on the bunk beside Callahan and interrogated him about the case. He told me about the plans, the names and addresses of the people involved, giving the main ones as Clyde Tinch, the preacher, Billy Joe Tinch, and himself.

For an hour or so I continued to question Callahan. Although I wouldn't admit it to myself, something in his frank, open recital impressed me. At the end of the interview I asked Callahan how he'd gotten started on this kind of life. It was the sad story of a fourteen-year-old introduced to crime by a brother-in-law who taught Callahan how to burglarize a house. "I wanted a bicycle. Stealing was the only way I knew to get the money to buy it."

By now he was pacing the cell, and I noticed that he limped. "There's one thing that is really eating my gut," he said. "I've done a lot of bad things in my life, but one thing I've never done is harm a woman or child. That story in the newspaper about me attacking a woman and kicking her baby is a stinking lie. I've always respected womenfolk."

For a moment Callahan's guard had come down and I saw in his passionate protest a new quality. A touch of yearning to be understood.

I put away my notes and papers and gave the young man instructions to do no more talking to reporters; the newspaper stories had been very damaging. Then I said something that surprised me: "You just tell me the truth and I will fight for you." I meant it. My mind had not quite accepted his story, but something deep inside me had been touched by this man.

Yet, I came away from my first conference with Callahan faced with one hard and disagreeable fact. In order to save the life of my client, it would be necessary to break down the testimony of a preacher who would be the prosecutor's chief witness against Callahan. As a minister, Clyde Tinch would have a lot of influence with a jury.

We lawyers cannot—actually must not—set ourselves up as judges. We are not to pass judgment but only to marshal our skills to present and test the witnesses and other evidence.

But in this case I would be going against a preacher. Although not a Christian, all my life I had feared the wrath of God if I should speak aught against the church or its ministers. So it was with real reluctance that I began digging into the background of Preacher Clyde Tinch.

My investigation of Clyde Tinch began with a call to the headquarters of his church denomination. Cautiously, an executive there answered a few questions, then referred me to two of their local churches where he had served as an assistant minister. I called on these pastors, each of whom gave me a frank report on the young preacher's service to the church. They in turn referred me to some of their leading laymen.

The picture that emerged of Clyde Tinch was a confusing one. He was a persuasive evangelist, he was married to a loyal Christian woman, and he had personal charm. It was alleged also that he was a hard drinker, had been dishonest in financial dealings, and consorted with prostitutes.

Such information is what the law characterizes as hearsay evidence, and of course is not admissible in court. But it did give me a hint as to the kind of person I was up against, and calmed my fears about having to attack his character on cross-examination at the trial.

Next I talked to the five detectives assigned to the case. They had uncovered no new evidence that would be damaging to my client.

Then I began the task of interviewing some eleven other witnesses expected to be subpoenaed by the State to testify in this case. This called for weary legwork, trudging up and down streets and back alleys, ringing doorbells, asking questions, ears always alert for a lead or a bit of information that would strengthen the defense.

In addition to discrediting the testimony of Preacher Clyde Tinch, I wanted to show that Callahan could not have shot the grocer because he was too drunk. One of Callahan's drinking friends with him the afternoon of the murder was a man named Fred Timmonds, a metal worker in the same plant where Callahan had worked.

When I called Timmonds for a conference, at first he refused to see me. Finally, he did agree to meet me at a bar. We sat down at a small table in a dimly lit tavern just off Trinity Avenue. Timmonds stared at me hard-eyed behind a stubble of whiskers.

"Tommy Callahan was drunk the day of the murder, wasn't he?" I began.

The man unbuttoned his leather jacket and took a gulp from his glass. "We were all drinking that day," he said noncommittally.

"But Callahan was too drunk to walk or drive a car, wasn't he?"

Timmonds shrugged. "I don't remember."

Further questions drew the same clipped replies. In frustration, I finally fired off this shot. "The prosecution has bought you off, Timmonds. You're afraid to tell the truth, aren't you?"

His fingers tightened around his glass, but he did not answer.

"When I see Callahan tomorrow I'll tell him what a great friend you are." I paid the bill and walked off, leaving Timmonds sitting there, cold, hostile, silent.

Others suspected of complicity in the robbery greeted me with the same set lips and defiant stares. They obviously considered Callahan a loser. But more than that, fear flickered behind every pair of eyes. From experience I felt sure they'd been contacted by the prosecution; even routine questioning by someone on the solicitor general's staff can rouse the specter of indictment if there is no cooperation. Some wit-

nesses probably hoped for special favors in the way of
forgiveness for past or present offenses in return for
helpful testimony for the State.

When I returned for my second visit with T. C. Callahan, however, I was feeling less pessimistic. The
case against him was not as clear-cut and overwhelming as the news media had reported. Again I questioned Tommy carefully about every detail of his
story. Satisfied that he had remained consistent, I dug
more into his background, his early years.

A lot of the tension seemed to drain out of the prisoner as he leaned back on his bunk bed. He began to
talk as one who desperately needed to empty himself
of a lot of painful memories.

"As far back as I can remember my family lived in
an old abandoned church out in the country. We were
too poor to rent a house. My father died when I was
about six years old and left my mother and us six kids
really bad off." He was silent for a moment, as if
struggling with feelings that had no words.

"Behind the old church was an apple orchard," he
continued. "This was our only food except for some
dry cornmeal. We bought the meal with money from
selling some of the apples down on the highway."

Callahan paused and looked at me soberly. "I don't
care if I never see another apple for as long as I live.
We ate baked apples, stewed apples, dried apples,
boiled apples, big apples, little apples, ripe apples,
green apples, even rotten apples!

"There was a chain-gang camp near this old church,

and early every morning the convicts and the guards would walk past the church, going out to work on the road. The convicts had chains on their legs, and the guards carried shotguns and had two large bloodhounds on leashes.

"One day a convict escaped from the camp and hid in our attic. My mother fed him and took care of him. Then she fell in love with this convict and they went to Atlanta and were married. Later they sent for us children.

"When I was nine and a half years old, the police picked up my stepfather and returned him to the chain gang. The depression was on, and we were worse off than ever. We had to go to the Salvation Army for food until I got a job delivering newspapers.

"I got up at one o'clock in the morning to deliver my newspapers, and then went to school. I earned $2.50 a week; it was a big help in those days. The route man would drive the car and I'd stand on the running board and toss the rolled-up papers on the porches of the customers.

"We were crossing an intersection one day when this truck came barreling through a stop sign. It hit our car on the side where I was standing. I was pinned between the car and the truck. I woke up in the hospital with a plaster cast over my entire body, except my arms. My skull and back were fractured, both legs broken, and my left foot crushed.

"I was in the hospital over twenty months. After getting out I wore a cast on my left leg for fourteen months. I still limp in that leg.

"When I got back home, Mother was bootlegging white liquor to feed us. When I was about fourteen, my older sister's husband took me out with him one night. We went to this house. He told me he was too big to squeeze through the small window. He showed me how to do it and then told me what to do inside the house. He waited for me in the car. I sneaked through the house while the people were asleep and stole jewelry and ladies' handbags."

"Did you feel that what you were doing was wrong?" I broke in.

Callahan reflected a minute before he answered. "For the first time in my life I had money in my pocket. I bought a bicycle. I never thought I'd have one. I had accomplished something. Sure I knew it was wrong, but I'd tried going to school and working hard and that didn't pay off. Robbing a house did."

"How far did you go in school?" I asked.

"Through the fourth grade. Then I started running around with a gang of guys older than me. We had our own burglar tools and went to the rich side of town and began robbing houses at night. We were caught and charged with thirty-one burglaries. Because of my youth I was sentenced to only two years.

"While in jail I got in with a tough crowd. After a few months some of us escaped. I went back to burglarizing and was caught again. As a second offender I was given twenty years in Reidsville State Prison."

Callahan stared moodily into space. "I got out on parole six months ago and decided I would stay out of

trouble. I was doing okay on my job. When Clyde
Tinch came to see me that morning I knew it was
trouble. I think that's why I got drunk. If I got dead
drunk, I couldn't be a part of it. And I wasn't, except . . ." He didn't finish.

"Tommy, there's one episode in that story I need to
know more about," I said. "After the murder you and
Billy Joe stole a car and drove out to Ohio. You abandoned the car in Cincinnati and hopped a freight to
Toledo. There in the freight yard you shot a police-
man. Why did you do it?"

Callahan's eyes had flashed a series of emotions as I
spoke—guile, fear, bitterness. Now there was a new
one—anger.

"I've always had a problem with my temper," he
admitted. "And that railroad guard made me mad.
Billy Joe and I were just standing there when this guy
came up behind me with his gun. I'm small in size and
have had to be tough to make up for it. This guard
says, 'Hey, Shorty, stand over against the wall while I
search you.'

"I pulled my gun and said, 'I'll search you!' He was
going to shoot me, so I shot first. One bullet hit his gun
belt and knocked him down. I turned to run and he
shot at me; I swung around and shot him in the leg—
and continued to run. I'm glad the guard wasn't badly
hurt. But he went after me first."

"By the way, Callahan, the trial is set for Monday,
November nineteenth. Judge James Ashley will be
presiding."

Callahan looked shocked. "Man, that's bad. When

Ashley was a prosecutor, he gave me twenty years for burglary. As judge—when he sees me again—he's not going to like me!"

Back in my office, I gave serious thought to Callahan's statement about Judge Ashley. As a prosecutor he had gained a reputation as a fearless pursuer of criminals, advocating stiff punishments as the only effective deterrent. He was aggressive and pugnacious, and fought like a bulldog, giving no quarter and asking none.

Just how impartial could Judge Ashley be now, with one of the very criminals he thought he'd put safely away? I decided to confront him with the question.

Several days later an appointment was set up for me at the courthouse in Judge Ashley's private chambers. He greeted me politely, then sat down at his desk. He was short and heavyset in stature.

"As you know, Judge, the Callahan case is coming up for trial the week of November nineteenth in your court."

He nodded.

"I'm sure that you are aware that Callahan was out on parole from a long burglary sentence when he was arrested and charged with murder."

"Yes." He began drumming his fingers on the side of his chair.

"Judge, I have just been advised by my client, Callahan, that as our former solicitor general, you prosecuted and convicted him in that burglary case."

"That's true, I did."

The judge sat there, waiting for my next question, jaw thrust out combatively. With a sinking feeling I sensed he would resent what I was about to say.

"Judge Ashley, because of these circumstances, I feel compelled to make a request of you. The code of the American Bar Association says that: 'A judge formerly employed by the State in another department of government should disqualify himself in a proceeding if his impartiality might reasonably be questioned because of such former association.' I am wondering if you would consider disqualifying yourself in this case?"

The judge's eyes bored into mine. "Mr. Bradford, do you question my fairness or my impartiality?"

"No, sir, I have the highest respect for you as a judge, and I greatly admired you as solicitor general."

Judge Ashley's stern features relaxed only slightly as I continued: "Here's the way I see it, sir. You are there on the bench, looking down on Callahan sitting at the defense table. Try as you will, you must remember him sitting in the same place when you prosecuted him for burglary and sent him up for a long stretch. Now, while out on parole, he has gotten into trouble and is before you again, this time charged with murder. It must cross your mind that, perhaps, if the Parole Board had left him where you put him, this murder wouldn't have taken place," I said.

Judge Ashley shook his head, and the fingers resumed their drumming. "In spite of all that, I would not allow this to influence my conduct on the bench. I

can and will be just as fair in this case," the judge
replied.

It was a futile effort on my part, but I made one last
thrust. "Your Honor, with no reflection on the
judiciary, the knowledge of the defendant's past
crimes carries with it such potential for bias that almost any judge would find it hard to maintain that
calm detachment necessary for fair adjudication. I
would urge you, sir, to comply with the spirit of the
ABA code by taking yourself out of this case and letting one of the other judges try it."

The judge's face darkened. "No, I will not disqualify myself. I do not feel that this circumstance will
hinder my ability to preside over the trial in an unbiased and unprejudiced manner."

A request like mine is up to the discretion of the
judge. When he refuses to stand aside, there is nothing a lawyer can do. I thanked Judge Ashley for his
consideration and departed.

I walked slowly down the corridor of the courthouse, with a deep sense of uneasiness about the task
before me.

# 4

# The Murder Trial

The morning of Monday, November 19, 1951, was cool and clear in Atlanta. I pulled the collar of my topcoat a little closer as I made my way along the windy street to the Fulton County Courthouse.

The courthouse is a mammoth, nine-story building, constructed in 1907 of Georgia-grey granite. Gripping my briefcase, I pushed open the heavy bronze doors and entered the lobby, always a scene of special tension on a Monday morning. Amid the sea of humanity were lawyers waiting for their clients, jurors and witnesses looking for the right courtroom, court attachés hurrying to their various assignments, and the merely curious who came daily to sit in on the drama of society at its worst. I've always felt that if the passion, tension, fear, hate, and frustration there on a given day could be harnessed in some way, it would blow the top off the courthouse.

An elevator took me to the sixth floor, and a walk

down a long corridor brought me to Room 605. I felt the familiar butterflies in my stomach—much as a prize-fighter feels on his walk from the dressing room to the ring.

Pushing open the swinging doors, I stepped into a pretentious courtroom paneled in walnut. Large gold-framed portraits of past jurists lined the walls. The spectators' section of a hundred and fifty seats was already filled, and there was a larger than usual representation of press reporters. Beyond a railing an inner court was reserved for the judge, the jury, the parties and their lawyers, the court reporter, the clerk of the court, and court attachés. I took my seat at the defense table in this inner section.

One of the bailiffs, noting my arrival, left the room by the rear door and soon returned with my client, Tommy Callahan. With little show of emotion Callahan crossed the room and sat down beside me. I was pleased to see that he had taken my advice, and was neatly dressed in a dark suit with white shirt and dark necktie. I wanted the defendant to look as credible as possible. To me, the solemnity of the courtroom is second only to that of the church.

Already seated at the State's table was the public prosecutor, Frank French. His wavy hair neatly parted, his tweed suit freshly pressed, he was clearly confident of victory. Flanking him were his top assistant, Carl Copeland, and three veteran police officers. We nodded to each other, not with hostility, but with mutual respect.

Then the court bailiff rapped loudly with his gavel and announced, "The Superior Court of Fulton County is now in session, the Honorable Judge J. E. Ashley presiding. Please rise."

The judge in his black robe walked in briskly, mounted the bench, and asked the people to be seated. The selection of a jury can be long and tedious, but this time we were able to complete it in an hour and a half. With the jury sworn in, the prosecutor outlined the State's case, calling sternly for the death penalty for Callahan. In my defense statement I announced that we would show that Callahan never entered the grocery store and could not have fired the murder weapon.

Judge Ashley said, "Mr. Solicitor, call your first witness for the State."

Solicitor French called to the witness stand Mr. R. E. Kilman, father of the victim: "Raise your right hand and place your left hand upon the Holy Bible. Do you solemnly swear that the evidence you are about to give, in the case of the State versus T. C. Callahan, charged with the offense of murder, will be the truth, the whole truth, and nothing but the truth, so help you God?"

With a dignified mournful clarity the witness replied, "I do," and sat down in the witness chair. Kilman was a slightly built man with sparse grey hair and rimless eyeglasses. His deeply wrinkled skin spoke of a lifetime of dawn-to-dark hard work.

The questioning by Solicitor French began in a routine way, the court stenographer recording:

"Mr. Kilman, tell us, what business were you in on July sixth of this year?"

"I was in the grocery store business at 46 Trinity Avenue."

"Did you have any partners in your business?"

"Me and my two sons were partners."

"Which one of your two sons was working with you the night of July sixth?"

"My son, Howard Kilman, was working that night . . . ."

"What, if anything, unusual happened there that night?"

"This thing took place after 10:00 P.M. . . . I went around the meat counter to check my meat. I had just come in off my vacation and I was looking in the bottom of my meat case."

"Did you hear any outcry?" asked French.

"Yes . . . my boy said, 'Look out, Dad . . . .'" Kilman's face was showing the strain of recalling that terrible night.

"Tell the jury what you saw."

"Two boys were standing at the checkout stand, right up against it. One had a shotgun and the other had a pistol."

"What was the man with the pistol doing?"

"He was shooting!" Kilman became visibly agitated at this point, and a murmur arose among the spec-

tators. With a scowl Judge Ashley banged his gavel for
quiet, and the questioning resumed.

"Mr. Kilman, will you give us a description of these
two men?"

"One of them had a shotgun. He was a very tall
man—not so heavy; and the one that had the pistol
was about my height."

"How were they dressed?"

"The tall guy had a white handkerchief from the
eyes down. The other had a black handkerchief on his
face."

"Since this terrible thing happened, have you seen
either of these boys?"

"No."

"Have you ever known a fellow by the name of Billy
Joe Tinch?"

"I knew Billy Joe Tinch when he was a small child,
but I had not seen him in some time."

"Do you know his brother, Clyde Tinch?"

"Yes."

"Did you ever know T. C. Callahan, the defendant
on trial?"

"No."

"State whether or not you could identify either of
the two men in your store that night."

"No, I would not want to do that. I know that one of
them was a tall man and the other one was more or
less my height."

"When you saw the men, what did you do?"

"I raised up and began to holler, for I knew they had shot my boy."

"Did you actually see them shoot your son?"

"Yes."

"What happened then?"

"The tall boy said, 'Let's get out of here, Claude,' and he ran out the door."

"What did you do?"

"I thought probably the man with the pistol would go out, but he came facing me and shot at me."

"How many times did this man fire at you?"

"He shot three or four times at me; he fired at my son three times."

"When the man began to shoot at you, state what you did."

"After he fired at me, I had my gun, and I shot at him."

When the old man reached this point in his testimony he began to sob uncontrollably. This time the courtroom was quiet, and Solicitor French waited until his witness had his emotions under control.

"After you fired at this man, what did he do?"

"He quit shooting and ran out."

"Then what did you do?"

"I went directly out the door behind the man."

"When you got outside, what did you see?"

"They were crossing Memorial Drive, right opposite my store, going down Crew Street. They were traveling in an old model car, black-looking."

"What did you do then, if anything?"

"I emptied my gun at them, and shook my fist, and dared them to come back!"

This produced a smattering of applause across the courtroom. The solicitor concluded his questioning by bringing out the fact that Kilman's son died from these gunshot wounds. Then he turned the witness over to me for cross-examination.

"Mr. Kilman," I began, "on direct examination you testified that the tall boy said, 'Let's get out of here, Claude.' Isn't that true?"

"Yes, the one with the shotgun made that remark."

"Mr. Kilman, in the terror of that moment, could you not have misunderstood the given name on the tail end of the remark by the bandit, and didn't he really say, 'Let's get out of here, Clyde'—instead of Claude?"

"Yes, sir, I was excited. I did not know but what my life would be next."

"Now, let's see if we can find out who 'Claude' is. One thing is certain, he is the killer. The defendant's full name is Thomas Cecil Callahan. The preacher's full name is Michael Clyde Tinch. Which one of these names phonetically sounds like Claude—Clyde or Cecil?"

"Clyde, of course."

The prosecutor was on his feet at once. "The question is objected to on the ground it is argumentative, speculative, and calls for a conclusion."

Judge Ashley's answer: "Sustained."

Having made the point, I was happy to withdraw the question and continue my interrogation of Kilman.

"Did the man with the shotgun fire it?"

"No, he was too scared."

"Then the man with the pistol murdered your son."

"Yes, he did."

"Now, let me ask you, Mr. Kilman, can you swear that the man with the pistol was not Clyde Tinch?"

"No, I do not know that it was not Clyde."

"Mr. Kilman, I want to ask you one last question."

I walked across the courtroom to where the defendant was seated and placed my hand on his shoulder. "Stand up, Callahan, and face the witness," I said.

"Now, Mr. Kilman, I want you to take a good look at T. C. Callahan. Take your time and study him from head to foot. When you have made up your mind, turn around and tell the jury if you can identify this man as the one who shot and killed your son."

There was a long moment of frozen silence in the courtroom at this gamble on my part. Even Judge Ashley looked startled. Mr. Kilman wrinkled up his forehead and peered over his glasses at Callahan for a moment. "I can't identify T. C. Callahan as being one of the men that entered my store, no, sir."

"I can't hear the witness's answer," I said to the court. "May I have the court reporter read it back?"

Judge Ashley said, "Will the court reporter please read the answer back."

"I can't identify T. C. Callahan as being one of the men that entered my store, no, sir." The loud voice of the court reporter rang through the courtroom.

Trusting the reply was doubly imprinted on the jurors' minds, I had no further questions.

At dinner that evening my mind was so preoccupied with the case that I scarcely responded to Thelma's attempts at conversation. Brenda had a slight cold, and she'd put her to bed early. A friend was getting a divorce. The clothes dryer had stopped working. Thelma had had a man out to inspect the dryer and he recommended we buy a new one.

Ordinarily, the need to purchase a new appliance would have had my complete attention. Not this evening. Finally, Thelma put down her fork. "Brad, we are not communicating at all. Is the case going badly?"

"No, I can't say that. But it's the most difficult case I've ever tackled. There's been so much destructive publicity about Callahan in the papers. One story inferred that he tore the clothes off a twelve-year-old girl and kicked a small baby she was holding. No truth to it whatsoever. But if the jury gets wind of these reports it would probably hurt him. French is going hard for the death penalty. I'm not to judge, but I don't feel Callahan is a murderer."

Thelma gave me a long, level gaze. "I believe Callahan has become a cause for you."

I pondered that idea. I hadn't seen myself as a

crusader—only a lawyer doing a thankless job for no pay because of his professional ethics. "You may be right. Something about Callahan has gotten to me. I don't want to see him die. There's good in him."

"Then you can be sure that God will help you see that justice is done," she replied.

"Callahan grew up without a father in such poverty that the only way he could have any possession of his own was to steal it."

Thelma reached over to touch my hand. "I'm glad you're defending this man, Brad."

Mollified, I squeezed Thelma's hand and headed for my briefcase filled with data on the case. Hours later, as I was getting ready for bed, I wondered again whether I was letting this thing turn into a cause. At all costs a lawyer must keep his perspective and not let emotion color his thinking.

Was I getting too involved?

# 5

## Witness for the Prosecution

The next three witnesses for the State added bits and pieces of corroborating evidence under questioning by the solicitor. Willard Dix testified that he drove the second getaway car, but thought that they were going to pick up some girls. He did not know the three men on the back seat of his car, except that one of the fellows called another "T. C."

Clifford Dix was under indictment and was not called, but Helen Dix testified for the State that she knew the whole crowd. She stated that they were all at her home drinking during the day of the murder; that Billy Joe Tinch was sawing off the barrel of a shotgun in the bedroom; that Clyde Tinch jerked the light fixture out of the ceiling so she couldn't see what they were doing.

When I cross-examined her she said that all of the men, including Clyde Tinch, had been drinking heavily, and that T. C. Callahan was slumped in a chair sleeping off a drunk. So far, none of the evidence was too damaging to my client.

Dr. Herman D. Jones from the State Crime Laboratory testified for the State that he had performed a post-mortem on Howard Kilman. The cause of death was excessive hemorrhage in the lungs from two bullet wounds.

Then at last the State called Michael Clyde Tinch. He was a handsome young man of medium height and build, with deep-set grey eyes and blond hair. All his movements, the inflection and timbre of his voice, even the prayerful clasp of his hands, were those of a clergyman. He stated that Billy Joe Tinch was his brother and that he had known Callahan for seven or eight years.

When asked his occupation, he said, "I am a part-time preacher and an inventory clerk for an auto-parts company. I have not been very active in the ministry recently, although my wife and I have been helping to establish a church in Brookhaven."

Queried as to what he did, beginning on the morning of July sixth, he gave a lengthy description of a trip to a union office and then to his mother's home, where he was to meet his brother, Billy Joe, who owed him money. Billy Joe didn't have the money, but promised to get it, and the two brothers then went to the home of Clifford and Helen Dix to meet T. C. Callahan.

"What was T. C. doing when you arrived?"

"T. C. was sitting in a chair in the corner of the living room. He had been drinking."

Clyde Tinch went on to describe himself as an onlooker while his brother and Clifford Dix obtained a pipe-cutter and hacksaw and sawed off the barrel of a shotgun. He then told how he, Billy Joe, and T. C. Callahan got into a car with Billy Joe driving.

"Then where did you drive to?" asked the prosecutor.

"We drove by the Kilman grocery store, and T. C. said there were four or five customers in the store, and to just drive on."

"Were you doing anything at that time?"

"I was asking to get out of the Plymouth."

"What did you say to Billy Joe?"

"I told Billy Joe I realized what was going on, that I knew what was up. I knew that both he and Callahan had been in prison . . . ."

I shot out of my seat. "If Your Honor pleases, I ask for a mistrial in this case! The State's star witness has placed the defendant's character in evidence by testifying that he has been in prison. The sole reason for this is to prejudice and inflame the minds of the jurors against Callahan."

Judge Ashley leaned forward. "I am going to overrule the motion for a mistrial, but I am going to ask you, gentlemen of the jury, to disregard the statement by this witness. Just eliminate it from your minds as if it had never been said."

But I pressed the point. "Your Honor, the prosecutor has deliberately led his witness's testimony, perfected by pre-trial rehearsal, to reveal the prison records of T. C. Callahan and Billy Joe Tinch. This places their characters in evidence, and I say again this is a ground for a mistrial."

I quoted from Georgia Criminal Law, Code Section 38–202: " 'General character of the parties and especially their conduct in other transactions are irrelevant matters . . . .' If Your Honor pleases, the damage has been done—no amount of persuasion by this good court can reach down into the brains and memories of these jurors and pluck out those prejudicial seeds. This is a life or death case, and all we ask is a fair trial not tainted by prejudicial matter."

Judge Ashley shook his head. "I do not think this witness has been induced to make the statement objected to by you. I am going to overrule the motion for a mistrial, and again instruct you, gentlemen of the jury, to disregard it entirely."

The questioning resumed, and Clyde Tinch described how Billy Joe drove the car in which he and Callahan were riding back to Kilman's store.

"T. C. got out of the back door and Billy Joe got out of the front door opposite the driver's seat," he said.

"Were these boys armed?" asked the prosecutor.

"T. C. Callahan had a pistol in his hand, and Billy Joe had a shotgun," replied Clyde.

"Where did Billy Joe and T. C. go?"

"They both went in the store."

"How long were they gone?"

"It seemed like they hardly had time to get into the store before the shooting started."

"What happened then?"

"Billy Joe came running back, slid under the wheel, and started the car up, and was moving away when T. C. jumped into the car. The back door was not shut, and it hit a parked car on Crew Street. We whirled back into Capitol Avenue and got away from there in a hurry."

"What happened then?"

"We parked the car about a half mile from there, on Berne Street, and Billy Joe got out of the car and told T. C. to watch me, that he would be right back. T. C. had a gun and told me to stay where I was. Billy Joe came back with the Dix boys in the other car, and T. C. was at my back with the gun and told me to get in."

"Name those in this second getaway car at this time," said the prosecutor.

"Willard and Clifford Dix were on the front seat, and me and T. C. Callahan and Billy Joe were on the back seat of the car."

"State whether or not there was any conversation between T. C. and Billy Joe immediately after leaving the Kilman store."

The part-time preacher cockily replied. "When they jumped into the car I heard T. C. say, 'I killed him, Billy. I had to.' Billy said, 'You are joking; you did not shoot him.' T. C. said, 'I did, too. I shot him three times.' Then Billy Joe said, 'If you had to shoot him, you could have shot him in the leg.' T. C. said, 'They had you in the crossfire and I had to do it.'"

Suddenly, there was a piercing scream from the spectator section. Everyone stared at a thin woman in a brown dress. Callahan's distraught mother received ministrations from the bailiff, while Judge Ashley rapped his gavel and the questioning resumed.

"Was there any conversation in the second car?"

"T. C. raised up and pointed the gun and said, 'I have just shot one man, three more won't make any difference.' Willard Dix jumped out of the car and ran back in the direction we had come from, and right there I jumped out, too!"

"Where did you go after you left the second car?"

"I ran down Berne Street and made my way to my sister's house. That is the same neighborhood. After I got there, Billy Joe and T. C. Callahan came in."

"When did you see Billy Joe and T. C. again?"

"The next afternoon, after work. That is the last time I saw them until they were captured by the police."

Solicitor French turned to me with a grin and said, "You may cross-examine the witness."

The testimony was damaging, and as I approached the witness I knew that the whole case depended on my tearing down Clyde Tinch's credibility.

"On the day of the murder, did you not go to the Lockheed bomber plant?"

"Yes, I went with a friend."

"Is it not true that you had already been fired by the Lockheed Company?"

"I had been dismissed out there as an unsatisfactory probationary employee."

"Now at the Dix home, after you watched them saw off the shotgun barrel, isn't it true that Billy Joe said to you, 'Clyde, you are taking a back step when you come in on this'?"

"It is not true."

"Isn't it true," I persisted, "that you then said, 'I don't care, I have got to have some money for my family'?"

"I did not make that statement to my brother."

"Isn't it true that Billy Joe said to you, 'Clyde, don't drink any of that stuff. You are going to have a lot of responsibility tonight'?"

"It is not true."

"You saw the shotgun being sawed off. Now explain to the jury the purpose of this."

"Yes, I saw the shotgun sawed off, but I didn't know the purpose, or what it was to be used for."

"Tell the jury what possible use Billy Joe could make of a sawed-off shotgun that night other than to rob or kill somebody."

"They are used for riot squads and things like that."

"Is Billy Joe a member of a riot squad?"

"No. Not that I know of," he replied lamely.

The response of the witness induced half-suppressed laughs from some of the spectators, which Judge Ashley's stern gaze over his glasses soon extinguished.

"Now, didn't Billy Joe tell you to be careful when you went in the store, that you might have trouble with that red-headed boy?" I pressed.

"No, I don't remember him saying that."

"Didn't he also warn you that this boy had been in the war, and he was tough?"

"No."

"Now, didn't you answer your brother, Billy Joe, with 'What is to be will be'?"

"That is a doctrine that was gotten up by one of our ministers."

"Didn't you go in the store and shoot that grocer?"

"No, I didn't."

"Now, when you and T. C. left the Dix house that night, he didn't have a pistol, did he?"

"No, he didn't have a pistol or a shotgun."

"You can't truthfully swear that you saw Billy Joe and T. C. Callahan in the Kilman grocery store, can you?"

"The obstacle between them and me was the partition of the store."

"You didn't answer my question. Could you see them in the store?"

"No, I could not see what went on inside the store. They were out of my sight."

"Now, in your written confession you said, and I quote, 'T. C. shoved a pistol in my side, bruising it, and said, "Keep quiet you s_____ of a b_____. Do as we say, or else." ' "

"When I asked them to let me out of the car the first time, that was when the pistol was drawn and placed in my side."

"Now, you stated to the jury just a while ago that when you and T. C. got into the car with Billy Joe, T. C. didn't have a pistol or a shotgun. Tell us, where did the pistol come from?"

"I—I don't know," he stammered.

Clyde Tinch was losing his ministerial composure, and at the prosecutor's table French was crossing and recrossing his legs.

I stood quietly for a moment, then asked, "Are you telling the jury that you were kept in the car by your own brother—against your will?"

"Yes, they kept me in the car against my will. The gun was trained on me while we rode back to the store."

"When Billy Joe and T. C. got out of the automobile in front of the Kilman store, did they take their guns with them?"

"When they went in the store, they carried their guns."

"Then you were left alone in the automobile, weren't you?"

"I was in the car alone."

"Now let's review your situation," I said with a glance at the jury. "You say that you had made two trips to the store with T. C.'s gun in your ribs, against your will, but now T. C. and the gun are gone and you are in the car alone—is that right?"

"There was no gun pointed at me at that time."

"Now, Mr. Tinch, will you please face the jury and tell them why—why you didn't scream out for help or just jump out of that car and run like the devil?"

The witness hesitated; the blood drained from his face. He threw helpless glances at the prosecutor.

"As to why I did not get out and run then—in the

first place, I was so scared I didn't know what to do."

"Could it be that you didn't leave the car because you were sitting under the steering wheel, waiting for your accomplices?"

"It is not true."

"Could it be," I pressed, "that you weren't in the car, but in the store with your brother, Billy Joe, and T. C. was passed out drunk on the back seat?"

The witness plucked at his necktie as though the knot were suddenly too tight.

"No—no—no."

"I believe it has been testified that after the robbery attempt was over, Willard Dix left the car first, followed by Clifford Dix. When did you leave the car, Mr. Tinch?"

"Soon after that. I came from the back seat and ran off down the street."

"When you ran away from the car, who was left then?"

"I left Billy Joe and T. C. in the car."

"Did you, as a man of God and a respectable law-abiding citizen, report the robbery-slaying immediately to the police, that night, or the next day, or the day after?"

"No, sir."

"In fact, you didn't say anything about the murder until after Willard Dix and Clifford Dix were arrested, and the police came out to your house the next week."

"Yes—yes, that's right, I was arrested on the ninth day of July, at my home."

"What were you charged with?"

"I was charged with aiding and abetting a murder."

"You were in jail only one day before you made your written confession against your brother, Billy Joe, and T. C. Callahan, saddling them with the crime, isn't that right?"

"Yes."

"I presume you were then let out of jail on bond, weren't you?"

"Yes."

"You are not under indictment today, four and a half months after the murder, are you?"

"No, I am not under indictment."

"Well, then, you are the only member of this gang that is free, aren't you?"

"That is true, as far as I know."

"Is this the immunity the prosecutor promised you for coming down here today and testifying?"

Prosecutor French came to his feet, protesting, "We object to the form of the question, Your Honor! There's been no testimony about immunity to anyone."

The judge sustained the objection. I turned back to the man in the witness chair.

"Mr. Tinch, are you an ordained minister of the church?"

"I am not a licensed minister in the church. I have held an Exhorter's license. But my membership is not with the church now."

"Mr. Tinch, you were quoted in the *Atlanta Journal*

newspaper on July eleventh that, 'The right will always win; the truth will never fail.' Tell us—please
tell the jury—what is the truth in this case?"

The preacher swallowed, started to speak, swallowed again. A full minute of silence elapsed. I
exulted in the witness's silence, for nothing creates
the aura of guilt more than refusing to testify under
oath in court. But the witness hung his head and sat
quietly, squeezing his hands.

I stared at him, then with all the contempt I could
put in my voice said, "You may come down."

Adjournment followed. I packed my papers in my
briefcase and started for the elevator. At the door of
the courtroom an attractive but very angry woman
confronted me. "You are a heartless person," she said.
"You have destroyed my husband's reputation and
character."

So this was Clyde Tinch's wife. She was a lovely
woman and, I had heard, a dedicated Christian. Now
her pretty face was clouded with humiliation and
grief.

"My husband and I are ruined. We will have to
leave Atlanta."

"I'm as sorry as I can be about that, ma'am. But you
have it wrong. I haven't ruined your husband's character. His character is what he himself has made it."

# 6

## The Verdict

The trial was resumed the next day. The final four witnesses called for the State were detectives with the Atlanta Police Department, who described their investigation at the scene of the murder, but did not include evidence against Callahan. The State rested its case.

My first witness for the defense was Frank Roberson, a driver for a laundry and dry-cleaning firm. He was a large, muscular man with an open face.

"Mr. Roberson, were you at home on the night of July sixth?" I asked.

"Yes, I was."

"Did anything unusual happen in front of your house that night?"

"Yes, after I had retired I heard a noise on the outside and a car door slam. I thought possibly it was my son, whom I was expecting. I looked outside and saw a car parked in front of my house, blocking my driveway."

"Was this your son?"

"No. I waited and watched for a second to see. Then I noticed two men pulling something out of the car. One man was still inside the car and the others were trying to pull him out. They finally got him out of the car and they said, 'You young squirt, come on, and let's get away from here.' "

"What happened then?"

"One man got him by one arm and the other by the other arm, and they went off towards Memorial Drive."

"As these three men walked away from the car, describe them and their positions to each other."

"When they walked away, the smallest man of the three was in the middle."

"What did you do upon rising the next morning?"

"I got up about six o'clock and read the morning newspaper. One of the first articles I saw was where there was a murder. I read down a little bit and they mentioned a car. I looked out the window and saw the strange car still parked out there. It wasn't the one described in the paper, but I thought it was odd they would leave it blocking the driveway and all, so I called the police."

I turned to Solicitor French and said, "You may cross-examine the witness." French showed little interest in Roberson. He asked a few perfunctory questions, then said curtly, "That's all."

I then called several minor defense witnesses. Mr. M. D. Crowe testified that he was Callahan's

employer at a local steel construction plant, that Callahan was a good employee and a hard worker, that
the plant was closed down in July for vacations, and
Callahan was due to return to work in August.

Mrs. Mollie Cumbo testified for the defense that on
the day of the murder she saw Callahan during his
walk with Billy Joe Tinch and he was so drunk that he
could hardly speak to her. She also testified that she
knew the preacher, Clyde Tinch, and that his character in the neighborhood was bad and she would not
believe him under oath.

I also produced as witnesses several ministers who
had known the part-time preacher. The first was the
Reverend U. D. Tidmore.

"Reverend Tidmore, please give us some of the
background of your ministerial qualifications and experience."

"I have been in pastoral work most of the time since
1923. For the past three years I have been pastor of
the Hemphill Avenue Church."

"Reverend, are you acquainted with Clyde Tinch?"

"Yes, I have known Michael Clyde Tinch five or six
years."

"Are you familiar with his general reputation and
character?"

"Yes."

"Is that reputation good or bad?"

"That reputation has been bad, I am sorry to say."

"Would you believe Michael Clyde Tinch under
oath?"

"I would not believe Michael Clyde Tinch under oath."

A stir went through the spectators in the crowded courtroom. I turned to Prosecutor French, "Do you wish to cross-examine the witness?" He shook his head, and Tidmore stepped down.

The Reverend G. M. Rex then testified that Clyde Tinch's character had been good until he began getting involved with the opposite sex. Since then his character had not been good. The prosecutor objected to that answer and the objection was sustained.

Then I called Mr. Lee Watson, the owner of a local bakery, to the witness stand.

"Mr. Watson, would you tell the jury what church you are a member of, and what offices, if any, you hold in that church?"

"I am a member of the Hemphill Avenue Church and Superintendent of the Sunday School, Chairman of the Finance Board, and a Trustee of the church."

"Do you know Michael Clyde Tinch?"

"Yes."

"Are you familiar with his general reputation and character?"

"Yes, I know his general reputaton and character."

"Is that character good or bad?"

"That character is bad."

"Would you believe him under oath?"

"I am sorry to say that I could not believe Michael Clyde Tinch under oath."

When the prosecutor waived cross-examination, I

requested a ten-minute recess to talk to Callahan and prepare him to take the stand.

Tommy Callahan began his statement to the jury by declaring emphatically that he was not guilty of the murder of Howard Kilman. Then he told the story of his painful childhood, much as he had told it to me. Watching the faces of the jury, I could see that some of them were touched.

Callahan then recalled meeting the Tinch brothers and described the drinking bouts they would have together. The reason he got so drunk the day of the murder, he stated, was because something inside him did not want to go through with the robbery. He came across very believably, I felt, as he told how he tried to offset his small size with a lot of bravado. He was always attempting to prove how tough he was, yet deep down he was sickened by his criminal life-style.

At the end he said soberly, "What I have told you is the truth. I did not kill that man."

The defense rested.

I started my closing argument to the jury by reminding them that T. C. Callahan had entered the trial "with the presumption of innocence in his favor, and this presumption remains with him until the State produces evidence beyond a reasonable doubt as to Callahan's guilt of the offense charged."

Next I pointed out that Mr. Kilman had been asked if he could identify Callahan as the murderer and he could not do so. Then I bore in on Clyde Tinch. "Gen-

tlemen of the jury, the State is counting big on Clyde
Tinch. Its case stands or falls on your belief in him.
Let us examine carefully the testimony of this
preacher. I suggest to you that this part-time preacher
could be the murderer himself!

"First, Clyde Tinch was fired from his job and
needed money for his family. He was at the house
where the robbery was planned. When Helen Dix
walked into the room during the sawing off of the
shotgun barrel, Clyde Tinch jerked the light socket
out of the ceiling to hide their nefarious designs.

"He, a preacher, was there for hours, drinking with
the rest of the gang. He rode in the car to the scene of
the robbery-murder. He was later arrested for aiding
and abetting in the murder. He would be on trial himself for his life if he had not conveniently agreed to
testify for the prosecution.

"Now, let us look at some of the contradictions and
flaws in his testimony. Clyde Tinch stated that he was
forced at gunpoint to go along with the others. But
when he was left alone in the car in front of the store,
as he so states, he made no effort to escape.

"Clyde Tinch testified that T. C. made this statement: 'I shot him three times. They had Billy Joe in
the crossfire and I had to do it.' Now remember, Mr.
Kilman testified that he saw the pistol man shoot his
son three times before he himself even reached for his
gun. There was no crossfire until after Billy Joe turned
and ran from the store. Mr. Kilman's testimony makes
a bold-faced liar out of Clyde Tinch!

"Clyde Tinch said that he fled from their car after the murder, leaving only Billy Joe and T. C. Callahan in the automobile. Frank Roberson, a completely unbiased witness, testified that he saw three men walk away from that same car, the shortest man in the middle, who had to be pulled from the car. Gentlemen, you have seen Billy Joe, Clyde, and the defendant, Callahan, here in court. You can readily note that Callahan is the shortest. This witness makes it clear that Callahan, the short man, was in a condition to need help walking.

"You heard several ministers of God and two church lay people swear on the Holy Bible that Clyde Tinch's character is bad, and they would not believe him on oath. The judge will charge you that, 'where the unworthiness of a witness is established in the minds of the jury, he ought not to be believed, and it is the duty of the jury to disregard his testimony.' Yet the prosecution has built its entire case on this pseudo-preacher. Gentlemen, in closing, let me say I have looked through my law books, trying to find a name for the State's star witness, Clyde Tinch, the alleged preacher, but they were of no help. But I did find a name for him in the greatest of all books."

I lifted up a Bible for the jury to see. Then I opened it to the Book of Matthew, chapter 27:3–5, and read aloud:

> Then Judas, which had betrayed him, when he saw
> that he was condemned, repented himself . . . Say-
> ing, I have sinned in that I have betrayed the inno-

cent blood . . . . And he cast down the pieces of
silver . . . .

I walked briskly toward the railing behind which
the preacher was seated, and with studied emotion
shouted, "This man's name is Judas Iscariot! He sold
out his blood-brother and his friend, Callahan, to
avoid a murder rap!" Waving the confession docu-
ment at him I said, "This is your thirty pieces of
silver!"

Tinch licked his lips and stared straight ahead.
Turning again to the jury I made a final plea for Callahan, asking them for an acquittal because the State
had not proved Callahan guilty beyond a reasonable
doubt. "I pray that you will show the kind of mercy to
my client which Clyde Tinch has not shown."

The faces of the jury were solemn. There was not a
sound in the court.

Prosecutor French approached the jury box to make
the closing argument for the State. "Gentlemen, this
has been a long and hard-fought case, and we thank
you for your patience. But murder is a very serious
business, and we have tried to bring to you all of the
witnesses who know anything about it. We have
placed on the witness stand some sixteen witnesses in
an effort to satisfy your minds beyond a reasonable
doubt as to the defendant's guilt—this we believe we
have done."

Then he summarized the facts of the killing, stress-
ing the testimony of a man of God who heard the defendant admit his guilt. "You know it must have bro-

ken the heart of Reverend Clyde Tinch to testify
against Callahan and his brother, but he had to tell the
truth.

"Gentlemen, the State doesn't believe that Callahan deserves any more mercy than he showed Howard Kilman. This was a cold and calculated trip they
made to the Kilman store. They went to rob and kill.
The maximum penalty is justified. The State asks for
the extreme penalty in this case—death in the electric
chair!"

Prosecutor French sat down. Judge Ashley's charge
and instructions to the jury lasted almost two hours,
and included explanations of presumption of innocence, reasonable doubt, credibility of witnesses, in-
toxication, direct and circumstantial evidence, accomplices, flight, admissions, and lengthy definitions
of conspiracy and murder.

Then he gave the jury the three forms of verdicts
they would be authorized to consider: "I charge you
that, if you have a reasonable doubt as to the defendant's guilt of the offense of murder as charged in the
bill of indictment, it would be your duty to give him
the benefit of that doubt and to acquit him.

"Now, gentlemen, in the event you should convict
the defendant of murder, you would have a right to
recommend the defendant to the mercy of the court.
And in that event the punishment received by the
defendant would be imprisonment in the penitentiary
for life. Without the recommendation, it would mean

the defendant would receive the extreme penalty of death by electrocution."

At 8:00 P.M. the jury retired to deliberate the fate of T. C. Callahan.

For the next four hours I drifted miserably about the courtroom and the corridors, too keyed up to leave the building, too tense to be hungry. Shortly before midnight, the foreman of the jury rapped on the door and advised the court bailiff that they had reached a verdict. Quickly, we were all back in our places in the courtroom. "Mr. Foreman," said Judge Ashley, "has the jury reached a verdict?"

"Yes, we have, Your Honor."

The judge continued, "Please turn the verdict over to the solicitor general and let him publish it."

Solicitor French walked over to the jury box and accepted the verdict. Then Judge Ashley turned to the defense table: "Will the defendant stand and receive the verdict?" I stood along with Callahan as Solicitor French read aloud the verdict of the jury.

"We, the jury, find the defendant, T. C. Callahan, guilty."

Guilty . . . just that. No recommendation. The sentence: *death!*

I stood with a sick feeling in my stomach. There was a stunned silence across the courtroom. Every eye turned toward Callahan to see how he took it. He glanced up at me, face impassive, and said in a whisper, "The jury was kinda hard on me. They mustn't have believed my story."

Judge Ashley addressed Callahan. "Do you have anything to say before I pronounce sentence upon you?"

"No, sir."

"If Your Honor please," I said, "may I, as counsel for the defendant, speak in his behalf?"

"The Court will hear from you, Mr. Bradford."

"I ask for mercy and a life sentence for Callahan. You are well familiar with the Georgia law on punishment for murder. Code Section 26–1005 says: 'The punishment for persons convicted of murder shall be death, but may be confinement in the penitentiary for life in the following cases.' The relevant one before you today says: 'If the conviction is founded solely on circumstantial testimony, the presiding judge may sentence to confinement in the penitentiary for life.' I plead for a commutation because this conviction was founded solely on impeached and discredited circumstantial evidence."

Judge Ashley drummed his fingers on the papers before him. Then he adjusted his glasses and looked down, first at me, then at Callahan.

"T. C. Callahan," he said, "the jury has found you guilty of murder. It is considered, ordered, and adjudged by the Court that you, T. C. Callahan, be taken from the bar of this court to the common jail of Fulton County, there to be safely kept until your removal to the Georgia State Prison in Tatnall County for the purpose of the execution of this sentence in the manner prescribed by law.

"And it is further ordered and adjudged by the Court that the Warden of the Penitentiary of the State of Georgia shall execute you, T. C. Callahan, by electrocution, as provided herein and by law, in private, witnessed only by your counsel, relatives, and such clergymen and friends as you may so desire within the walls of said institution on the eleventh day of January, 1952, between the hours of ten o'clock and two o'clock P.M. And—may God have mercy on your soul."

# 7

# You Are Going to Die

The following week I visited Callahan at the Fulton Tower Jail to see if he wanted me to file a motion for a new trial. His eyes lit up when he saw me approach.

"I think that you have grounds for a new trial, and I'll go ahead with the paperwork if you want me to," I told him.

"Will it do any good?" he asked.

"It might. The evidence against you is weak. I just don't think the verdict can stand up."

"Mr. Bradford, I have no money to pay you."

"Tommy, we're talking about your life. The finances are my problem, not yours, and I'm not about to desert you now," I replied.

"Thanks for sticking by me—I do appreciate it—more than you'll ever know."

Thelma was right about one thing, anyway. Callahan had become a cause.

I filed our motion for a new trial and later our brief of evidence and amended motion. Judge Ashley au-

tomatically granted Callahan a stay of execution pend-
ing the outcome of our action. When the original date
for Callahan's execution—January 11, 1952—passed
by, I relaxed a little.

Meanwhile, the trial for Billy Joe Tinch was held.
His lawyer didn't place him on the witness stand, and
Billy Joe received a life sentence.

The trial of Clifford F. Dix was set for Monday,
January 16, 1952. I attended, hopeful that I might pick
up something new and material that would be helpful
in my motion for a new trial for Tommy Callahan.

Billy Joe had not been allowed to testify at Callahan's trial because he was scheduled for a trial of his
own, but after being sentenced to life imprisonment
he had nothing to gain or lose by his testimony in the
Dix trial. I listened hopefully when the defense counsel called Billy Joe to the stand and asked him for his
account of the murder.

"I was at home when my brother, Clyde, came to
see me," Billy Joe began. "He told me he was broke
and his wife and kids had nothing to eat in the house. I
let him have eight dollars, and he said that wasn't
enough, and he asked me did I know any way to make
any money.

"And I told him, well, I could help him get hold of
some money if he was willing to do certain things to
get it. And Clyde said he didn't care what he did to get
it. Clyde and I went to Clifford's house, and when we
got there we found T. C. Callahan passed out drunk in
a chair. I went across the street and got a shotgun and

a hacksaw, and Clyde held the gun while I sawed it off.

"Clyde and I got T. C. in the car with us and went to Mr. Kilman's store to hold it up. Clyde and I both had on masks and sunglasses. We pulled up in front of Mr. Kilman's place, and Clyde and I got out. We had the masks on. T. C. Callahan was in the car. He was drunk. We went in the place . . . ."

Startled, I lunged forward in my seat, blood pounding against my temples, every nerve in my body tingling. Here was precisely what Callahan had been claiming all along! Now we had new sworn evidence of the fact that the preacher, Clyde Tinch, went into the store with Billy Joe and not Callahan. Surely this was grounds for a new trial!

Billy Joe continued, "We went in the place, and when we came back out I jumped under the steering wheel, and Mr. Kilman was still shooting when we pulled off. He shot at us as we pulled across Memorial Drive.

"Clyde, my brother, went with me into the store. T. C. Callahan never did go in the store. I had been in Mr. Kilman's place before, and at times he had a right smart amount of money in the cash box. Clyde said he didn't care how we got the money. He needed some money for his wife and kids; he didn't have nothing to eat in the house."

On cross-examination by the prosecutor, Billy Joe testified: "I do not feel bitter toward my brother, Clyde, I love my brother; I love him now. The fact that he testified against me didn't make me feel bitter toward him. Just the fact that he said he didn't go in there; he was telling a lie about it. He said he didn't, but he did. I am not angry at Clyde."

At the trial's recess, I went to the court reporter and requested a transcript of Billy Joe's testimony, together with his affidavit. Armed with these I appeared in Judge Ashley's court on a cold, raw morning—February 4, 1952—to argue our motion for a new trial.

I had barely started to speak when the judge's fingers began their familiar drumming. To the accompaniment of his tattoo I made my appeal for a new trial, based on eight special grounds; the last was the newly discovered evidence that: "Billy Joe Tinch, the brother of the State's chief witness, has recently testified in court under oath that T. C. Callahan could not have killed the grocer because he did not enter the store."

The attorney representing the State made counterarguments—that Billy Joe was lying to get even with his brother and help his accomplice, Callahan, and could not be believed because he was a convicted felon.

After hearing our arguments, Judge Ashley, without any comment, grimly overruled our motion for a new trial. Then he gathered his black robe about himself and disappeared into his private chambers.

In some ways, Judge Ashley's curt refusal to grant a new trial was harder to understand than the guilty verdict. A clue to his attitude had appeared in the

*Atlanta Journal,* I recalled, the day after the trial closed. Back at my office, I dug the clipping from my files and read it again.

> Fulton Superior Court Judge J. E. Ashley turned down a plea for mercy and a life sentence from Callahan's court-appointed attorney, Kermit C. Bradford. The attorney asked for commutation on grounds the evidence was wholly circumstantial, thereby making the death sentence discretionary instead of mandatory upon the judge.
>
> Judge Ashley declared that the certainty of punishment is one of the strongest deterrents to crime. He said that on a recent trip to England he found that Fulton County had more murders than that entire country. "The reason England has so little crime is because punishment is certain," he declared.
>
> Reviewing Callahan's long criminal record, the judge noted that Callahan was sentenced in 1943 to 20 years for burglary. "Had Callahan been kept in jail, his sentence would not have expired until 1963 and he would not have been free to murder Mr. Kilman," the judge declared.

I appealed Judge Ashley's decision to the Georgia State Supreme Court by filing a bill of exceptions from the order overruling our motion for a new trial. Along with this I filed a written brief of evidence with citations of authorities.

When the case was called by the Supreme Court, I presented an oral argument before the justices. The

State again made its counter statement. No decision is delivered at the hearing. The justices always take the case under consideration.

On May 12, 1952, I received a letter from the Supreme Court of Georgia. I was surprised to find my hands shaking. I tore the letter open and scanned it swiftly: ". . . denied."

On June 25, 1952, Callahan and I faced Judge Ashley again for resentence. We stood there under an almost visible shroud of gloom as the judge in a monotone tolled off the death sentence for the second time.

That night, during a very quiet dinner, I could hardly swallow my food. Restlessly, I walked into the den, flopped down in my favorite chair, and picked up the newspaper. After a minute or two I tossed it aside.

Thelma came in and put her hand on my shoulder. "Do you want to talk about it, dear?" she asked.

"There's nothing to talk about."

"Yes, there is," she said gently. "You don't usually leave a nice steak almost untouched on your plate."

"It's the Callahan case—the State Supreme Court denied my motion for a new trial—and Judge Ashley has just resentenced him to die—sixteen days from now."

Thelma put her arms around me. "You've put your heart in this case, and I'm proud of you—I have a feeling that you'll think of something."

Four days later Thelma and I arrived at Mama's

small frame house at 10:30 A.M. to take her to church. Being the daughter of a country preacher, attending church with her family on Sunday was important to Mama, and it was seldom enough that I found time to do this small thing for her.

As we walked down the aisle of the Wesley Memorial Methodist Church, Mama, at seventy-one, was still a striking woman with her nobility of spirit and a love for all mankind. Her copper-colored hair was now speckled with gray.

Seating myself between these two women of strong faith, my thoughts went to Callahan. A man who was going to die in twelve days needed the kind of faith Mama and Thelma had.

At dinner, afterwards, I asked Mama if she remembered that I had defended young Callahan in a murder case.

"Yes, I've heard you speak of him."

"Well, he has been sentenced to die in about two weeks."

"Oh, I'm so sorry," she said sadly.

"Mama, he is not a Christian, and I thought perhaps you could recommend a preacher who would talk to him about his soul and prepare him to die."

"Yes, I know the very man," she said.

"I have no idea what Callahan will do," I said. "He may reject the whole idea. I don't think he's ever been inside a church—except the abandoned church building he grew up in. Who's the person you're thinking of?"

"His name is Bradley," she said. "Jim Bradley. He used to be the bell captain at the old Piedmont Hotel, furnishing liquor and women to guests. Then he was saved, and started attending Toccoa Bible Institute. Now he's an evangelist. Wherever there's a human need, Jim will go any time of the day or night."

"When I see Callahan tomorrow," I decided, "I'll ask him to let me bring Mr. Bradley over to pray with him."

"Son," said Mama gently, "be careful that in your desire to save the life of that young man, you don't forget your own spiritual need. When you were a little boy I dedicated you to God, and I have been praying ever since that you would really give yourself to Him."

I was deeply moved by her moist, pleading eyes and answered, "Oh, don't worry about me, Mama. Everything is going to be all right." Later that day I wondered why I had spoken those words, for I didn't have the answer—yet.

Monday morning I visited Callahan in Fulton Tower. He sat on the bunk, clean-shaven, hair well-groomed as always. I found it difficult to be as indifferent to his fate as he appeared to be.

"Tommy," I said, "let's have a serious talk. Now that you have been resentenced, any day now you'll be taken to the State Prison in Reidsville. There is one more thing I'd like to do before you go."

Tommy's eyes were trustful. "What is it?" he said.

"Will you let me bring a minister to pray with you? You need to make preparations to meet God's judgment in the spiritual world."

"Mr. Bradford, I don't know anything about preachers or religion. They never showed any interest in me. But you have. Will you pray for me?"

I was caught off guard. "Me? Well, I . . . I'm sorry I can't pray for you . . . because I'm a sinner, too . . . it would be an act of futility. Sinners can't pray for each other . . . you need a Christian to pray for you, one who is a worshiper of God and does His will." (*See* John 9:31.)

I wet my lips. "The fact is, Tommy, I haven't thought about God too much. I have been too busy all my life trying to be a success. I've always figured there was time for that later, but for you, well, there isn't any more time."

We were both silent for a while. "All right, Mr. Bradford, you can bring a preacher to see me. I'll listen to him."

I called Jim Bradley that night, and he said he'd be glad to visit the prisoner. The next morning I waited for him at the front gate of the Fulton Tower. Jim was in his early forties, of medium height, with a long neck and small head, wearing a poorly fitting blue suit and clutching a tattered Bible under his arm. I was not impressed—until I found myself looking into the warmest pair of eyes I'd ever seen.

As we ascended in the elevator to the maximum security floor of the prison, I briefed Bradley on Cal-

lahan's background. I thought he might be put off by
what he heard, but when the guard had locked us in
the cell and departed, Bradley went straight up to Callahan and embraced him warmly. Callahan, looking
embarrassed, sat down on his bunk while Bradley and
I stood.

Without preliminaries, Bradley began to probe in a
gentle way, trying to gauge the depth of what he assumed would be Callahan's contrition.

Opening his Bible, Bradley read aloud the story of
Creation, the account of Satan's entrance into the
Garden of Eden, and the disobedience by which
Adam and Eve frustrated God's perfect plan for His
world. "Things have gone wrong on our planet ever
since that first act of disobedience, Tommy. The rest
of the Old Testament describes how the children of
Adam and Eve struggled with Satan for thousands of
years.

"But Satan has always been too strong for us. And
so, God, in His infinite love sent Someone stronger
still." Turning to the New Testament, Bradley read
aloud from John 3:16: "For God so loved the world,
that he gave his only begotten Son, that whosoever
believeth in him should not perish, but have everlast-
ing life."

Callahan's eyes were fixed upon Bradley with sober
attention. "Tommy," Bradley continued, "your counselor tells me that you are not a Christian, and that you
are going to die in less than two weeks. I can tell you
two things for sure: first, when you sit in that electric

chair, you will not black out into oblivion or nothing-
ness. When God created man, He created him for
eternal life. You will live forever somewhere, be it
heaven or hell.

"Second: if you sit in that electric chair *without*
accepting Jesus Christ as your Saviour and Lord, your
eternity will be spent in hell. Now that sounds harsh, I
know, but I'm not here to play games with you. I'm
giving you the truth as it is in the Bible."

He found the thirteenth chapter of Matthew and
read:

"The Son of man shall send forth his angels, and
they shall gather out of his kingdom all things that
offend, and them which do iniquity; And shall cast
them into a furnace of fire: there shall be wailing and
gnashing of teeth."

Then Bradley turned ahead a few pages. "The Bible
says in John 3, except you be born again, before you
are executed, you cannot see or enter the kingdom of
God. I'm afraid that this leaves only hell for you.

"But, Tommy, this same book proclaims the infinite
love and mercy of God toward men. Jesus' death and
resurrection means that wicked, fallen men can be
restored to the very fellowship with their Creator
which they had in the beginning." Bradley flipped
through the dog-eared pages again. "Your hope is here
in Romans, chapter ten: 'For whosoever shall call
upon the name of the Lord shall be saved.'

"Jesus Christ loves you, Tommy. He doesn't want
you to go to hell. He wants you to be saved. God offers

you a pardon—it is free, but not cheap, for it cost God
His only Son on the cross.

"Think of it! The sins, the guilts, the failures of a
lifetime can be forgiven in a single moment of time. If
you are tired of crime and sin, and will here and now
place your faith in Jesus Christ and call upon Him to
forgive you and save your soul—He will do it."

There in the cell of a condemned man, I was a spectator to an extraordinary tug-of-war for a human soul.
On the one side was God's eloquent man, Jim Bradley. On the other, an invisible but malevolent force
which I could almost feel in the air.

Suddenly, Bradley stopped talking and bowed his
head in prayer. For a moment time seemed suspended
in that cell. Then, suddenly, the battle was over. As I
stared at Callahan's face, the doubt, the fear, the eva-
siveness vanished. Perhaps at that instant the criminal
died and the new man was born. In the hush of that
moment, without a word, Callahan slipped from the
edge of his bunk to his knees, next to Bradley. "God,
please forgive me for my sins . . . and make me different . . . and save me for Jesus' sake."

Not until we had retired for the night did I feel like
telling Thelma what happened. "Are you asleep,
honey?" I asked.

"No."

"I took Mr. Bradley over to the jail today."

"What happened?"

"Callahan got down on his knees by his bed and

asked Jesus to save him." I was glad it was dark, because my eyes were suddenly wet.

"That's wonderful, dear," she whispered.

"By the way, honey, when were you, er . . . saved?" I asked, stammering a bit over the often-heard phrase of my childhood.

"When I was ten. It happened at a meeting at the Methodist Church in Perry, Florida. I went forward to the altar and gave my heart to Christ . . . it was a big moment," she replied.

"Well, I went to the altar of our church a couple of times when I was a boy, but nothing happened," I said. "I'm still waiting to be convinced."

"Maybe we should go to church more often, Brad," Thelma answered.

"I live a decent life. I gave up that wild crowd the day I met you. I give to a lot of charities. What will an hour in church on Sunday do for me?"

"But, honey, don't you see, you haven't given up anything for Jesus," she replied gently.

I was stumped for an answer.

Thelma was silent for a while. "Maybe the real issue isn't church, but Jesus," she said at last, so softly I could barely hear.

I lay on the pillow, staring into the dark, thinking about her remarks and the extraordinary experience at the prison that morning.

# 8

# The Jurors Speak Out

Reidsville Penitentiary, two hundred miles south of Atlanta, is surrounded by a high, chain-link fence and concrete watchtowers manned by armed guards. Inside the fence, an enormous four-story building contains acres of cell blocks and workshops. A small fifth floor, reached only by an elevator, is octagon-shaped and houses Death Row.

The State of Georgia has put more men to death than any other state in the Union—a total of 415 executions, one of them a woman. Yet, the death sentence has been given to only a small percentage of convicted murderers in Georgia. In 1951, for example, five men had been sentenced to the chair, four for murder and one for rape. In that year Georgia recorded 636 criminal homicides.

Callahan was assigned to one of the five cells on Death Row, just a few feet from the execution chamber itself. When one of the inmates is "under a date," as penal jargon has it, he then goes to visit "old sparky" or "ride the thunderbolt," and the faint odor of charred wood pervades the whole of the cramped fifth-floor area.

With time running out, my next move had been to try to persuade the State Pardon and Parole Board to commute Callahan's death sentence to life imprisonment. As a first step I had visited the Board's office in the State Capitol and talked to Board member Charles W. Patrick. I emphasized the need for prompt action, as my client was due to be executed on Friday morning, July 11. I understood Mr. Patrick to say that he would set the case down for a hearing before the full Board on Monday, June 30, at 2:30 P.M.

On June thirtieth I arrived at the Pardon and Parole Board office ready to argue the case. Mr. Edward Everett, Chairman of the Board, a gentlemanly individual with a touch of gray at his temples, greeted me with a look of surprise. He had not been told of any hearing. When I explained the urgency of the situation he said that since Mr. Patrick and Mrs. Rebecca Garrett, the other two Board members, were in their offices, he would call them together and hear me.

A few minutes later Mr. Patrick appeared, frowning. "We cannot have a hearing without someone from the solicitor's office present. Why didn't you notify them?"

Fighting down my irritation, I replied, "Mr. Patrick, you said that you would handle all details when you set up a formal hearing here at 2:30 today."

"I never said that at all," he snapped.

"I'm sorry, but that's what I thought you said."

A barrel-chested man with a penetrating voice, Charles Patrick took a step closer. "I told you we would hear the case. Because you thought the hearing was today is your mistake, not mine!"

I wasn't going to be intimidated. "A man is due to die in the electric chair in a few days," I said. "I'm battling to save his life because I'm convinced he is not the murderer. You said you would set up a hearing and you haven't done it."

My anger had carried me too far. Patrick tore off his coat and raised his fists threateningly. "You've put my integrity in question, Mr. Bradford, and I won't take that from anyone."

I, too, shucked off my coat and stood there with fists cocked. It was a ridiculous scene, and I knew it, but if it had to come to a fight, I was ready. Mrs. Garrett looked on with a disbelieving expression as Mr. Everett stepped between us. Everybody sat down, and I tried to retrieve the situation with an apology to the Board. "I'm sorry about this. When you're fighting for a man's life you're under a great deal of pressure."

In the end, Chairman Everett called for a full Board hearing on Callahan's case on Tuesday, July 8, at 10:00 A.M. I had one week to file an application and serve a copy on the solicitor general, notifying him of the hearing.

It was hardly a victory, and I knew it. One Board member was now totally hostile to me, and the other two were unlikely to be sympathetic. Nothing seemed to go right in this case.

The night after my near fistfight at the Parole Board office, Mama was rushed to Grady Memorial Hospital with a severe asthma attack. I got there as soon as I heard. She was lying on a high hospital bed, pale and obviously in pain, but determined, as always, not to talk about herself. "Son, I've been praying for that man whose life you are trying to save."

Breathing was too difficult for her to go on talking, so I simply sat beside her, reaching for her hand when the spasms were bad.

While trying to comfort her, I recalled another time when Mama's prayers saved a life—my life—in an airplane crash. As a young man I had taken up flying in an open-cockpit plane. One day my plane developed engine trouble over a forest. The motor coughed, then stopped. Desperately, I looked below for some open space where I could land. There was none. As the trees came rushing up at me I started to call out to God for help. Yet, even in those fearful seconds before the crash, I felt that since I had not made a personal commitment to God, even though I was a church member, I had no right to call on Him. But I knew someone who could get an instant answer to her prayers.

In pure desperation, as I headed into the trees I found myself crying out, "Mama, if you've ever prayed for me, you'd better pray now!"

The plane slammed into the top of the trees with an ear-splitting crunch, and a big limb shot through the cockpit. It missed me by an inch, and like some giant supporting arm, held the plane where it was, and kept it from crashing through to the ground below. Releasing my safety belt, I climbed down through the branches to the ground without suffering even a scratch.

That evening I started to tell Mama about the plane crash. She interrupted me, "Son, I knew all about that last night."

I stared at her in astonishment. She continued, "Jesus came to me last night about midnight and woke me from a deep sleep. He told me that you were going to be in a crash and that He would take you away from me. I slipped out of bed, fell to my knees, and prayed for an hour. Jesus did not answer. I prayed another hour—He was still silent. I prayed the third hour, and still no response from my Lord.

"Then I said to Jesus that I had been on my knees for three hours and was very weary, but that I would not get off my knees until He promised me that He would give you another chance. Both He and I knew you weren't ready to meet Him face to face.

"Finally, Jesus spoke gently to my heart and said that there would be a crash, but that He would bring you through it and you would not be harmed."

I listened in utter amazement to Mama's words. But I didn't doubt a word she had said. Now, years later, as I listened to Mama's heavy breathing on the hospital bed, I wondered if her prayers for Callahan would be as powerful as they'd been when I, too, seemed headed for certain death.

The next morning I awoke with a wild, improbable idea that just might result in a commutation of Callahan's death sentence. Why not make personal calls on the jurors who brought in the guilty verdict against Callahan to see if they might now recommend clemency?

I tried the idea on a few friends, and all were intrigued; no one could recall it ever having been done before. With only nine days left before Callahan's electrocution, what did I have to lose?

My secretary, Margaret Lawton, obtained the names and addresses of the jurors, and on the evening of July second she and I started making our calls, taking along a portable typewriter and the notary public stamp which would make official any sworn affidavits we obtained. I had no idea what kind of reception we might receive.

The first man we called on was Walton O. Godby. I had barely launched into an explanation of the purpose of our visit before he was nodding his head vigorously. "I will certainly give you a statement, since I have been deeply troubled about the sentence given Callahan. I was the last juror to agree to the guilty verdict . . . ."

In his affidavit which Mrs. Lawton typed out on his living room table, Mr. Godby stated:

"I most earnestly recommend to the State Pardon

and Parole Board that Callahan's sentence be commuted to one of life imprisonment for the following
reasons:

"The other jurors told me that if Callahan was given
life, he would automatically be released at the end of
seven years. After much persuasion I finally gave in to
the other jurors, but have regretted it ever
since . . . .

"From the evidence presented I firmly believe that
the so-called preacher [Clyde Tinch] was the actual
triggerman . . . that Callahan was passed out drunk
on the back seat of the car and did not go into the
store.

"The way I feel about this case was brought to the
court's attention immediately after the verdict was
rendered, but the judge failed to act upon it."

Mr. Edmont Riser was the next juror we called
upon. As the foreman of the jury, his affidavit was
especially significant:

"As foreman of this jury, and after further consideration of this case, I now most earnestly recommend . . . that Callahan's sentence be commuted to
life for the following reasons:

"I do not believe he went into the store and committed the murder . . . .

"The jury did not convict him as the killer, but on
the grounds that he was one of the conspirators . . . .

"I felt the preacher [Tinch] was just as guilty as
Callahan . . . .

"I do not feel Callahan should receive a harsher

sentence than the others." (Two received life, Clyde Tinch no sentence at all.)

During the following three evenings we talked with five more of the jurors. All were eager to sign an affidavit asking that Callahan's sentence be changed to life. One admitted that his decision to vote guilty was based on the testimony that Callahan had a previous criminal record. Another felt that significant evidence had been withheld from the trial. Most stated that they felt Clyde Tinch was the actual killer.

Of the twelve jurors we tried to see, two had moved to other states and three were away on vacation. Yet seven affidavits out of twelve for a change of sentence made me jubilant.

The hearing was held on Tuesday morning in the walnut-paneled courtroom of the Pardon and Parole Board in the State Capitol. The three Board members sat on a raised platform facing the participants in the hearing, Chairman Edward Everett in a tall, leather chair in the middle, Mrs. Rebecca Garrett to his right, and Charles Patrick to his left. A court reporter was present to take down the proceedings. I was there representing Callahan, and Carl Copeland, the assistant solicitor general, represented the State.

The atmosphere was charged, with everyone aware that Callahan would die in seventy-two hours unless the Board changed the sentence. I introduced Keeler McArthur, a crime reporter for ten years with one of the local newspapers. He testified that he and a police captain were the first to arrive on the scene of young Kilman's murder. McArthur met two men who had been standing at the door of the grocery just as the two gunmen dashed out. I pointed out that these important witnesses had been permitted to leave town by the State because their testimony would apparently have been favorable to Callahan. This produced a vigorous denial by Mr. Copeland.

Several ministers appeared voluntarily and asked for clemency for Callahan. Then two members of Callahan's family made an emotional plea for his life. Letters were read into the record from concerned citizens pleading for mercy.

The faces of the Board members were immobile. It was time to play my ace. Pulling out the folder of affidavits, I placed it in front of the Board.

"Last week I interviewed seven of the twelve jurors who turned in the guilty verdict for Callahan. They eagerly signed affidavits requesting a change of sentence from death to life imprisonment; they also state their convictions about a miscarriage of justice in this case."

As I read aloud some of the affidavits I could tell by the sharp interest of panel members and the agitation of Mr. Copeland that we had scored.

The members of the Board asked a number of questions. Mr. Copeland objected to the "unorthodox" procedure. Both of us gave our closing arguments. The Board announced that they would take the case under advisement and let us have their decision not later than the next day. I went away from the hearing with high hopes.

Wednesday afternoon the decision from the Board was hand-delivered to my office. Scarcely breathing, I opened the letter and read:

> After a review of the brief of evidence and the information obtained at the hearing, the members of the Pardon and Parole Board arrive at the following conclusions:
>
> (1) Callahan did conspire and participate in a premeditated plan to rob a citizen by the use of deadly weapons which resulted in the death of the victim;
>
> (2) There exist no mitigating or extenuating circumstances sufficient to justify a modification of the death sentence imposed; and
>
> (3) Callahan was represented by able counsel and was not denied any of his constitutional rights.
>
> Therefore, it is considered, ordered, and adjudged that the application for commutation be denied.

Denied! That word again. Once again I had lost. I had lost the trial; I had lost the motion for new trial; I had lost the appeal; and now I had lost the hearing to the Pardon and Parole Board. And Callahan was due to die day after tomorrow!

I had one hope left: Governor Herman Talmadge. Under the laws of the State of Georgia, the governor has power to temporarily reprieve or suspend the execution of a sentence of death, after conviction, for purposes deemed necessary by the governor. This would give me time to prepare and present a writ of certiorari to the Supreme Court of the United States, my final effort.

I put in a call to the governor's office. A woman's voice answered: "I'm sorry, the governor is out of town—he should return Friday morning."

But 10:00 A.M. Friday was execution time! I hung up the phone in despair. "Will I ever get a break in this case?" I wondered bitterly. "I've never tried so hard and never failed so miserably."

Friday morning I was up early, determined to be sitting on the governor's doorstep when he arrived at the State Capitol. If he didn't arrive by 9:30, Callahan was a dead man.

At 7:30 A.M. I parked my car near the Capitol. As I crossed the plaza I stopped and looked pensively at the great Capitol dome adorned by a woman's statue fifteen feet tall. Perhaps she represents justice, I thought. Callahan could use a little of that right now.

I walked up the steps of the Capitol, past the six stone pedestals at the entrance, and hurried down the corridor to the governor's office. The door was locked. Restlessly, I paced the halls, pausing from time to time to stare unseeingly at the displays of flags and other memorabilia of the Civil, Spanish-American, and World Wars.

At 8:30 A.M. I was back at the governor's office just

as his secretary arrived. Quickly, I explained the urgency of my mission.

"The governor arrives between 9:00 and 9:30. I will make sure you are the first to see him," she promised.

The minutes ticked away on a large clock in the reception room. What if the governor is held up somewhere? What if he has an errand on the way?

People dropped in, talked to the secretary, drifted out. Some took seats in the reception room, like me, waiting for the governor. The clock ticked on. 9:15 . . . 9:20 . . . 9:25 . . . .

At 9:30 I had begun to sweat when the secretary crossed the room to tell me I could see the governor. He had apparently slipped in some back way.

Margaret Lawton had gone to the Reidsville State Prison to stand in for me with Tommy Callahan while I made my appeal to the governor. She reported to me later that by 9:15 A.M. the executioner had tested the electric chair for proper voltage and was ready. Chairs had been arranged for the expected overflow of witnesses, and the adjoining morgue made ready to receive Callahan's body.

Callahan himself was sitting on his bunk in the cell next to the execution chamber, reading his Bible and waiting. Mrs. Lawton was allowed a few minutes to talk and pray with him, followed by Bradley. Callahan said with a smile, "Mr. Bradley, I want you to know that I'm ready to go."

It was now past 9:30 A.M. Callahan asked Bradley to preach at his funeral and to walk beside him when the guards arrived.

"You have faith and courage, Tommy," said Bradley.

"Jesus will be walking with me," said Callahan. "He is here right now." Then he added, "When they ask me for my last statement, do you know what I am going to say?"

"What?" asked Bradley.

"I am going to tell them they are killing an innocent man."

The witnesses filed into the execution chamber and took their seats. The chaplain and the physicians were in their places, the executioner and two guards behind the electric chair. Captain W. T. Wallace, in charge of the execution squad, looked at his watch. It was nearly ten o'clock, the hour set for the execution.

As I hurried into Governor Herman Talmadge's office, he rose, extended his hand, and shook mine warmly. Tall, slender, and tanned, the governor had the look of an outdoorsman. His dark brown eyes were friendly.

As quickly as I could I related the high spots of Callahan's trial, the motion for a new trial, the appeal, the hearing before the Pardon and Parole Board, and the execution set for this morning. Placing before him the corroborating papers, I asked him to stop the execution so that I might have time to appeal the case to the Supreme Court of the United States.

The governor looked through the papers carefully as I kept glancing at the clock. It was almost ten o'clock. Finally, the governor looked up.

"Counselor, I commend you on the thorough way you have handled this court-appointed case." He went on to talk about the importance of lawyers giving their all to indigent cases, while the perspiration oozed from my body.

"I hate to interrupt you, Governor," I cut in. "They are probably ready to proceed with the execution of my client. If you don't pick up that phone and call them right now it may be too late."

He nodded, reached for the telephone, and put through a call on his direct line to the execution chamber in Reidsville Prison. I held my breath as the phone buzzed endlessly. Then I heard a voice answer on the other end.

"This is Governor Talmadge. Let me speak with the warden or the person in charge of the scheduled execution of T. C. Callahan." Now we were down to seconds!

"Hello, Captain Wallace? . . . yes . . . I'm glad it is not too late to stop the execution. Attorney Kermit Bradford is here in my office, and I'm granting him a stay of execution for thirty days, so that he can carry his appeal to the Supreme Court of the United States. I will send Warden Balkcom a confirmation of this order. Thank you, Captain."

The governor hung up the telephone and turned to me with a smile. "I trust, now, that justice may be done."

I don't remember how many times I thanked him, or how long I shook his hand. I left his office in a daze, feeling as if I had been the one saved in a last-minute reprieve.

Only minutes before Tommy Callahan was to leave his cell for execution, Warden Balkcom himself appeared at the door. "Tommy, I have good news for you—you have a thirty-day stay. Governor Talmadge just called and stopped the execution. Your lawyer is in his office right now."

Callahan later described to me his reaction: "The only window in the death cell is high and near the ceiling. Suddenly, I had a great desire to see outside. I jumped up on my toilet seat. By standing on tiptoe, I could just see out the window. Everything out there seemed more beautiful than it had ever been before in my life. The sky was bluer, the clouds whiter, the trees taller.

"I could hear inmates down in the prison yard, counting off for their daily work assignments. I said to myself, 'They don't know how lucky they are! I would take a life sentence right now and work in the rock pile every day of it.' That's how precious life is."

It is a paradox that man has to face death before he can appreciate the value of life.

# 9

## The Last Seat

I began at once to prepare our petition to the U.S. Supreme Court. I knew the odds were still against us, but I couldn't let that deter me.

My other major concern was Mama's health. She was still in the hospital with her asthma. On bad days she would have difficulty in breathing. During her good days I would find her up and about, ministering to the needs of other patients in the ward.

My mother had been in the hospital almost two weeks when Thelma and I stopped in together one evening. Mama was sitting up in bed, her beautiful, long, red hair freshly brushed, her face bright and smiling. When she saw us, she exclaimed, "I have good news—I'm going home in the morning! The doctor is amazed at the improvement. I'm breathing absolutely normally!"

Delighted, I told her I would arrange to come and take her home.

"This means that I can go to Indian Springs next

week," she continued. "I wish you'd both come with me."

Suddenly, my defenses were up. This religious conference was an important yearly event for Mama, but the revival camp meeting wasn't for me. "Mama, Thelma's not going to be here next week. She's taking Brenda to Florida to visit Aunt Deb. And I need every minute I can find to prepare the Supreme Court writ."

A strangled cry from across the hall made all of us turn our heads. "That dear, poor soul!" Mama said. "She has such terrible attacks of asthma that sometimes she tears all her clothes off, trying to breathe. I've spent hours talking and praying with her, but she's in such physical agony she can't think straight. I've asked Jesus that before my condition gets that bad, would He please come and take me home with Him some night in my sleep."

When the visiting hour was over, I kissed Mama good-bye. "I'll see you in the morning," I said. There was such a quiet, serene happiness surrounding her that I commented about it to Thelma in the parking lot. "Did you notice Mama's face when we said good-bye?"

"She looked . . . radiant," she said.

"I thought so too . . . but I saw a kind of mystical white glow illuminating her face like a light. When I kissed her, I looked in her eyes and had a strange feeling she was . . . not only looking at me, but her eyes were looking through and beyond me."

It was a few minutes past 3:00 A.M. when the telephone rang. "Mr. Bradford, your mother has taken a turn for the worse. Better come to the hospital as soon as you can."

Minutes later I hurried into Mama's room. No one was there but Mama. Her eyes were closed, a little smile on her face as though she were having a pleasant dream. I walked quickly over to the bed and touched her cheek, and I knew at once that Mama had left our world far behind her.

"I'm going home in the morning," she had told us—and she had—to that mansion in heaven she had talked about so much. I sensed this, but not being spiritual, I didn't understand.

Grief like a tidal wave swept my soul. Suddenly, I was her little boy again—just we two alone—as I sat down and took her hand in mine and wept. "Oh, Mama, let me tell you once more how much I love you and respect you.

"Forgive me for the times I took you for granted— for the times I was too busy being a success to think to tell you or show you how much you meant to me." Oh, such yearning love I had for her at the moment.

My grief turned to precious memories. The hymns and spiritual songs she sang as she went about her housework still echoed in my heart. I kept staring at her. Mama's face had been deeply traced by the suffering trials of life and carved by the fires of her spiritual experiences. Now these lines were overshadowed by an expression of supreme tranquility.

Later, I sat in the doctor's consulting room and listened to the unusual facts about Mama's medical situation. Her chart showed that she had been perfectly healthy except for the asthma, that she had responded well to treatment, that her condition had cleared up so completely that she was to be discharged that morning.

The night before, she had eaten a good supper and showed no adverse symptoms of any nature. During the night, nurses had gone through the asthma ward, checking on the sleeping patients. The first two bed checks indicated Mama was sleeping and resting well. During the 3:00 A.M. check the nurse observed that her blood pressure was dropping fast and her heart slowing down. The doctor on duty was summoned and immediately put into operation the procedure for heart failure. Nothing availed, as her bodily functions simply slowed down, then stopped.

I asked the question that was most important to me. "Doctor, from the time my mother went to sleep, did she ever wake up, did she gain consciousness while the doctor was working on her, did she know she was dying?"

The doctor replied, "No," to all three questions and added, "It was very unusual. She didn't even give a sigh. We can't say what was the cause of her death, but we can say that she didn't die from asthma."

An autopsy was performed, and they did not find a single disease, injury, or breakdown in her body. Listed on her death certificate under cause of death was: UNKNOWN—with a large question mark!

I didn't believe in miracles, but here was factual evidence to satisfy my legalistic mind that Mama's last request and prayer had been answered.

In the family room of Patterson's Funeral Home on Spring Street, where she lay, there was only a sense of quiet repose. The great reservoir of her spiritual strength was stilled. I had lived these many years in the presence of spiritual greatness—and like most sons had taken it all for granted.

Mama had constantly challenged my inner man for something far greater than surface success, something the world can't give or take away. She wanted for me no great accomplishments of skill, only a simple bending of my will. And I failed her.

Losing Mama and feeling my inadequacy to save the life of Callahan shook my belief in my own invincibility. For the first time I felt my helplessness and admitted to myself that perhaps I needed help above and beyond myself.

Then a startling realization flooded me. Mama had left this world in peace—as if she knew that her work was done. She had departed with a sense of victory, not defeat. Chills raced up and down my back. That last night she had looked right through me and saw something that seemed to please her very much. Had she a glimpse of something still in the future?

Fearful that with the passage of time her influence might fade away, I felt compelled to take a new step for me. In the privacy of the family room, I dropped to

my knees beside Mama's casket and promised her that
I would really try to find God.

Lights burned late in my office in the days that followed as we began the long, drawn-out process of
preparing our writ of certiorari. Mrs. Lawton and I
spent much time in the Federal Law Library reading
through federal decisions on civil rights, conspiracy
against the rights of citizens, deprivation of rights
under color of law, and equal protection of the law.
The U.S. Supreme Court will not exert its jurisdiction
merely to review a decision of a State Court upon a
question of fact alone. There must also be a federal
right involved; we wanted to show a violation of Callahan's rights under the Fourteenth Amendment to
the Constitution.

On Sunday morning, several weeks after Mama's
funeral, the house was quiet except for the sound of
my sandaled feet as I headed for the kitchen to make a
cup of coffee. Thelma and Brenda had gone to Perry,
Florida, to be with Thelma's aunt. Restlessly, I
browsed through the morning paper.

Then once again thoughts of Mama tumbled into my
mind. I recalled the Bible stories she had read to me
as a child. The Christian life she had lived before me
daily was a continuing sermon that spoke to my heart
more eloquently than the greatest oration. The memory of her faith was like an anchor holding me close to
God. During the summer months she had so loved to

attend camp meetings where the "old-time" religion
flourished and where she spent hours in travail at the
altar, praying for my salvation.

Suddenly, I realized that today was the final session
of the annual Indian Springs Camp Meeting held at
Jackson, Georgia, which she had so counted on attending. Out of grief and loneliness I made an impul-
sive decision to go to this place that had meant so
much to her. It was only about seventy-five miles
south of Atlanta; I could be there in a couple of hours.

Indian Springs Holiness Camp Ground has an old,
shingle-roof, open-air tabernacle and a circle of
weathered wooden lodges surrounded by beautiful
old trees. When I arrived a service was already under
way and the tabernacle was crowded.

In the center of one row I saw a single empty seat. I
sat down, congratulating myself on finding the last
seat. Then I turned and saw that the seat to my right
was also vacant, although no one had left. I could have
sworn that somebody was sitting there.

"Mama?" I said in confusion, for I suddenly had an
overwhelming sense of her presence there beside me.
I was not the emotional type—I did not think that men
should cry in public, yet at that moment tears of joy
flowed down my cheeks.

The sermon was the usual sort of thing I'd sat
through as a boy. The preacher closed with an invitation for any to come forward who'd been "convicted of
sin." I'm afraid I didn't hear a single word the
preacher said. I just sat there and reveled in silent

devotion with the memory of Mama's faith and love. I
sat back to wait until the altar call was over, intending
to quietly slip out.

The next instant I was standing in the aisle, halfway
to the altar! I remember looking back over the sea of
faces at the two empty seats, wondering how I had
gotten out here. It was as though a giant hand had
picked me up out of my seat and was now propelling
me forward.

I struggled to regain my rational, thinking self. But a
Voice inside me was saying, "You have come seeking
fulfillment for your life—it is here. If you turn away
this time, you will never come again; the desire will
be quenched."

All at once I was driven forward by my desperate
need of Jesus to fill the emptiness in my life and—let
me be honest about it—my subconscious fear of suffering in hell forever if I didn't. I distinctly felt that I
was walking to my judgment as a condemned sinner.
This was no religious experience to me—this was
sober reality! The soul is always a battleground. Ordinarily you do not make an all-out decision to commit
your life to God without some agony and a desperate
need. When you make up your mind to follow Jesus, it
can be a lonely place.

I dropped to my knees at the altar and prayed sin-
cerely for the first time from my heart. "God, I come to
You because the world does not have the answer to
life. I am at the end of myself. I throw myself on Your
mercy and confess that I am a sinner. I ask Your for-

giveness, and if You will hear me, I accept with all my heart, Your Son, Jesus Christ, as my Saviour and Lord. I give You my life to cleanse and use as You will, for Jesus' sake."

My search was over!

On October 27, the writ of certiorari for T. C. Callahan was presented to the Supreme Court of the United States. It was considered and denied.

On November 4, Judge Ashley for the third time issued his sentence for Callahan to die in the electric chair at the Georgia State Prison. The date— November 21, 1952.

Thus, the clock of death was wound up again and began ticking off the time. Callahan had thirteen days to live. The U.S. Supreme Court was the end of the legal road.

At the office I sifted aimlessly through the mountains of accumulated documents on the Callahan case. I had never felt more helpless in my life. "What do we do now?" I asked Mrs. Lawton.

Without a minute's hesitation, she replied, "We can pray."

And we did, right then. It was a new experience for me to admit my helplessness so openly. Yet, doing so made me feel free. The weight was off my shoulders. If I no longer carried the burden, who did? God? That thought somehow staggered me.

This was only one of several changes I'd noticed taking place in me since that decision at Indian

Springs. The most startling were changes in actual body chemistry. Most males, for example, have a roving eye for an attractive woman. At least, I'd always told myself this was a normal reaction.

Several days after the Indian Springs experience I was walking down Peachtree Street when I noticed just ahead of me a beautiful blond young woman in an extremely short skirt. I could tell from the stares of other men that her seductive message was being received. But to my surprise my emotional response was not lust, but compassion. Could this be Kermit Bradford thinking and feeling, or was it a new person? If I was a new person, how, exactly, had this come about?

Ever since that weekend in the cabin when I had taken my first drink of whiskey, I had fitted myself into the world of social drinkers, careful to know my capacity, determined never to make a fool of myself. I took an occasional bourbon and ginger ale after work. I would sit in my large, overstuffed chair in the living room before dinner and hold the glass in my hand with keen anticipation. My mouth would water so that I could almost taste the bourbon before I drank it.

The first night following my trip to Indian Springs, I came home after work to an empty house. Thelma and Brenda were not due back for another week. I mixed a bourbon and ginger ale and sat down in my chair. But something was very different.

My mouth was dry. No desire for the drink. This was not something in my mind, this was a physical change in my body. Waves of mixed feelings flushed through me. I was beginning to feel something *new* inside me. It is an intuitive thing I cannot explain, a change of character, something that I had no control over. I was more than a rehabilitated sinner, I had received a whole new life with new desires and controls—a rearranged set of values. (*See* 2 Corinthians 5:17.)

This was why the feeling of lust was gone, why I had lost my taste for bourbon. And as the weeks and months passed, other temptations of the flesh strangely lost their attraction. Through the mystery of "Christ living in me" I had miraculously acquired a love in my heart for all people, and had rejected sinful habits in the same way a body rejects an alien heart transplant. (*See* Galatians 2:20, Colossians 1:27.)

The next week I met Thelma and Brenda at the airport and said nothing about my experience at Indian Springs to Thelma until after dinner. But I caught her looking at me quizzically several times. The right moment came in the kitchen. Brenda had been put to bed and Thelma was setting the table for breakfast.

"I went to Indian Springs last Sunday," I began in a voice that was suddenly husky with emotion. Thelma looked up at me quickly, and her eyes began to fill with tears. Her sensitive spirit seemed to know what I was going to say before I said it. When I told her of my kneeling at the altar she quickly responded, "I knew something had happened as soon as I saw you. It was written on your face." We soon were in each other's arms.

# 10

## The Dying Place

As Mrs. Lawton and I reviewed each step of the Callahan case, I came back again to the one group who still had the power to do something—the three-member Pardon and Parole Board. They had denied us before on a 2–1 vote.

"If one person on the Board changes his mind, then would Callahan be saved from the chair?" Mrs. Lawton asked.

I nodded. "I think Mrs. Garrett voted for us. Mr. Patrick was so angry at me that I doubt he could ever be won over."

"So that leaves the chairman, Mr. Everett."

"That's right."

"But how can you get another hearing?" There were only ten days now until the scheduled execution.

How indeed? "The only way I could persuade them to meet again would be to come up with some new evidence."

Once again I went back to the same dreary neighborhood and sought out the same people who had been so guarded with me before. It was disheartening. Fear, suspicion, and hostility still registered in every face. The first day, nothing. The second, nothing. Two more days, and still not one single scrap of new evidence. A week passed.

On the eighth day I wearily trudged up the front steps of the house next to the Dix home, and punched the bell button on a paint-peeled door. Mrs. Willie Mae Vernon answered my ring. She brushed back a wisp of gray hair from her face as I explained my visit, then she invited me in. Seated in her cluttered living room, once more I patiently explained that a man who I felt was innocent of murder would die in the electric chair in two days unless I could come up with some new evidence.

Mrs. Vernon's care-lined face was twitching as she stroked the arm of her worn brown armchair. "I don't think T. C. was in on the robbery," she suddenly blurted.

"Why do you say that?"

"Because I overheard the Tinch brothers planning the robbery that day when I went over to borrow Helen's vacuum cleaner, and Callahan was not there."

I leaned forward in my chair. "Will you be willing to sign a statement to this effect, that T. C. Callahan was not a part of this planning discussion?"

Mrs. Vernon's eyes clouded. "I don't want to cause anyone any trouble."

"Oh, you won't cause any trouble; you will be a help to see that justice is done."

Mrs. Vernon's conscience was obviously troubling her, but she was in a state of indecision. In the past I would have pushed her hard. Now, to my own surprise, I found myself putting no pressure on her. Instead, I prayed silently.

A few minutes later Mrs. Vernon said, "I guess I should help you . . . ?"

At once I called Mr. Everett of the Parole Board and requested a special emergency hearing on Callahan. "I have obtained a sworn statement by Mrs. Willie Mae Vernon, who overheard the plotting and planning of the Kilman robbery," I said. "I feel strongly that this throws enough new light on the case as to justify another hearing."

There was a long silence. I reminded Mr. Everett that Callahan was due to die day after tomorrow.

"All right," he said. "Be in court tomorrow afternoon at 3:30."

Strangely enough, as the execution date approached I no longer felt the pressure as I had before. It had been lifted along with the anxiety. This new Christian philosophy of life was beginning to take over. Yet, I had to face it. My presentation would be as weak as anything I had ever put together in my entire legal career. All I had was one woman's negative testimony that she had heard the robbery being planned, and that T. C. Callahan was not a part of the discussion.

The next morning a letter arrived from Callahan. "Hi Brad," it began. "This will be the last letter I'll ever write in my life . . . ." Tommy then went on to pour out his gratitude for my efforts and to discuss his funeral plans; his family had arranged for a hearse to bring his body back to Atlanta, instead of the usual burial on prison property. "Brad," he said in closing, "would it be possible for you to be with me on my last day? I would like to have someone to pray with and talk to at the end."

Callahan didn't know of the Parole Board hearing, and it was just as well. There was no point in having his hopes raised on the flimsy new evidence I was presenting. I made plans to drive to Reidsville right after the hearing.

When I arrived at the hearing room that afternoon, I was surprised at the composure I felt. Weak as my case was, I was strangely relaxed. It was as if the whole situation was out of my hands.

I began my presentation by reading Mrs. Vernon's letter to the Board, and once again briefly outlined and reviewed the entire case.

After listening patiently to me, the Chairman of the Board assured me they would again take the case under advisement and let me hear from them. I pointed to the clock on the wall of the hearing chamber and said, "There isn't much time left. When this hearing is over, I'll be driving to Reidsville. Callahan has requested that I come and walk the last mile with him to the electric chair in the morning."

As I stood before the Board I felt a power and confidence I had never felt before—that God was really there. At the very end I made one last statement, almost as an aside, which I had not planned to say.

"Whatever the outcome of this hearing, there have been two good results from this very involved case. Tommy Callahan has accepted the Lord as his Saviour, and just recently I, too, found Jesus Christ as my Lord and Saviour. I'm grateful to the Board for your patience with me in having this second hearing."

It was 10:00 P.M. when I checked into a motel that night at Reidsville. I was up early the next day and arrived at the State Prison about 8:00 A.M. There was to be a double electrocution that morning, due to begin at 9:30. In the courtyard of the prison I spotted the long, black hearse waiting to receive Callahan's body.

I was checked through the main gate and escorted by a guard to the warden's office. As we entered his office, Warden Roger Balkcom was removing some object from the lower drawer of a cabinet. He turned, and I saw in his hands the death helmet Callahan would wear—a macabre-looking object.

Hastily handing it to an assistant, the warden asked me to sit down. "I won't be attending the execution," he began. "It tears me apart. Captain Wallace will be there to supervise things."

"I can understand that," I said. "If Callahan hadn't made a personal request, I wouldn't be here either."

"I try not to let my feelings get involved with these men," the warden continued. "But I have to tell you that Callahan is the most unusual man we've ever had on Death Row. He has certainly found help in his religion, hasn't he?"

"How do you mean?"

"Most condemned men go through a grisly time the night before they die. They sometimes scream, they curse, they bang their bodies against the wall, and they throw their food on the floor.

"Not Callahan. Last night we gave him the usual privilege of ordering whatever he wanted for dinner. He asked for a steak, medium rare; mashed potatoes and gravy; several vegetables; corn bread; an ice-cream sundae; cake; and coffee. John Smith, the other prisoner who is to die this morning, also ordered a meal, but when both trays were delivered, Smith said he couldn't eat. So Callahan asked the guard if he would eat with him.

"The guard, Sam Billings, is a kindly old-timer. He pulled his chair over to Callahan's cell and sat outside the bars with Smith's tray on his lap, while Callahan sat inside with his tray. Callahan asked the blessing and then the two of them scraped their plates clean."

I shook my head in wonder. "That's real peace of mind and heart."

"Early this morning we prepared the two men for execution," the warden continued. "We gave them a shower and clean clothes. We asked if they had any last requests. Callahan said, yes, he certainly did. His

pants were too big and baggy, and his shirt had stain
marks on the front. He wanted to die feeling clean and
properly dressed.

"That really got to me," the warden continued. "I
told the guards to follow Callahan's instructions to the
letter. Then he asked one more favor. 'Please let me
walk to the execution room by myself. Ask the guards
not to hold on to my arms.' When I suggested that he
might need some assistance, he shook his head.

" 'I will have some assistance. Jesus will be with
me.' "

Warden Balkcom sat silently for a moment, staring
out the window. Then he looked at his watch. It was
almost nine A.M. "Mr. Bradford, I believe you want to
see Callahan for a few minutes before we begin the
proceedings."

He called in a guard, who escorted me to an
elevator. We stepped out on the fifth floor, and I got
my first look at Death Row. To my astonishment, the
elevator opened directly into the execution chamber.
The guard paused to lock the elevator door behind us,
while I looked apprehensively about. The high-
ceilinged white room was damp and chilly with a
smell of disinfectant in the air. Chairs and benches
lined the walls, but the huge, unpainted, wooden
chair in the center of the room, with its apparatus of
hardware and wires, drew all my attention.

I knew something of the history of this chair. When
Georgia turned from the practice of hanging to electrocution, in 1924, the state did not own an electric

chair. The first man to be condemned under the new law, a twenty-year-old black man named Howard Hinton, said that if timber were brought to his cell in the old prison farm in Milledgeville, he would build a chair. The materials were delivered, the prisoner constructed the chair, and on September 13, 1924, became the first man to die in it. Since then 414 others had followed him to eternity from the same contraption, the chair being moved here to Reidsville in 1937.

The guard tapped me on the arm and we crossed the room. To my right I caught sight of the morgue, with its embalming table and the six-foot-long drawers where executed bodies were stored until disposition. We passed a telephone on the wall, and I reflected ruefully that it had once rung in time to save Tommy Callahan—only to put him through this agony a second time.

The guard unlocked an iron door and led me along a narrow walkway into the cell area. The ceiling of this "final walk" was open with iron bars across it. "This is their last view of the sky," the guard explained.

Tommy was sitting on the bunk in one of the five cells, reading the Bible. In accordance with the warden's instructions, he was neatly dressed with a close shave and carefully combed hair.

"Hello, Tommy," I said. "The warden gave me special permission to come up and see you."

Tom's eyes lit up with real joy. "Hi, Brad," he said, "I'm glad you're here!"

What do you say to a young, healthy man who is about to die?

"I'm sorry, Tommy. I've done everything I know how to do."

"Don't feel bad, Brad. You've done more than you think. You not only kept me alive for a year—you got me introduced to Jesus."

With a wistful smile he added, "In a way, I'm lucky. I've been forced to face up to death. The people on the outside of these walls don't know when they will die, and most of them won't make preparations."

Then Callahan introduced me to John Smith, the other condemned man in the adjoining cell. He was a black man who had been convicted of murdering a man in Savannah.

It was a strange new role for me—to play a chaplain role to two dying men. "John, do you feel your life is in proper order?" I asked hesitantly.

"I've accepted the Lord and am ready now to meet Him," he replied promptly. Then John began to hum an old Negro spiritual "Swing Low, Sweet Chariot." He had a deep, resonant voice, and the words sent chills shooting through my flesh:

> I looked over Jordan and what did I see?
> Comin' for to carry me home,
> A band of angels comin' after me,
> Comin' for to carry me home.

The words flowed softly through the cell area, then stopped. I was too choked to say anything.

Callahan broke the silence. "Ever since the day you brought Mr. Bradley over to the jail in Atlanta to pray for me," Tommy went on, "I've been reading the Bible and praying to God. John and I are both ready to go. We know Jesus is with us and we'll be with Him in heaven in just a few minutes."

I asked the two men if they would like to pray, and they both said yes. The three of us got down on our knees, each of them at the corner of their cells, I on the outside. I reached through the bars with my right hand and took the hand of John Smith and with my left hand grabbed Callahan's. It was the first prayer I had ever said out loud with other people. It was probably stumbling and incoherent, but it was spoken from the heart. When I finished, John asked, "Will you stay with us to the end, somebody who cares about us?"

"Yes," I nodded—my voice cracking.

Then my ears picked up the whine of the elevator rising to the fifth floor. Captain Wallace and his execution squad would be on it.

I was still on my knees talking to the two men when the heavy iron door to the cell area clanged open. A hand fell on my shoulder, and Captain Wallace said, "It's time. Will you please proceed to the execution chamber, Mr. Bradford?"

I said a final good-bye to Callahan and John Smith. As I stepped outside, Captain Wallace said, "I hate to subject you to a double ordeal, but Smith is scheduled to go first. It's hardest on the one who goes second, and well, Callahan seems better prepared, somehow. Do you think you can take it, Mr. Bradford? There's no way out. The elevator is locked on the first floor until after the execution."

"Don't worry, Captain, I'll find a place over in the corner, out of the way," I replied.

But looking around the crowded execution chamber I saw that all the seats were taken except one. The two physicians, the chaplain, the witnesses, and a number of newspaper reporters were seated along the wall. The remaining empty chair was directly in front of the electric chair with only six feet of separation.

Reluctantly, I sat down, wishing desperately that there was some spot for me farther away—far, far away. A guard standing near me leaned over my shoulder and with an insensitive attempt at humor whispered, "Counselor, when it happens—don't puke!"

Captain Wallace, four guards, and a prayer-murmuring chaplain entered with John Smith. The black man was clutching his Bible.

John slowly looked at all the faces in the high-ceilinged white room until his eyes met mine. There was a flash of recognition and a faint smile. After handing his Bible to the chaplain, he walked to the big wooden chair perched on its rubber-carpeted platform, and sat down.

Working rapidly, the guards began fastening the leather restraining belts around his waist, arms, and legs, binding him tightly to the chair. As the executioner attached the electrodes to the calf of John's right leg, I was engrossed in watching the doomed man. He seemed completely absorbed in what the executioner was doing. There was no fear on his face as the shallow container which housed the other electrode was fitted to his head and buckled under his chin. The whole procedure took about forty seconds. I could feel the tremendous tenseness in the room. I was benumbed by this awesome sight of a man all trussed up and about to die!

The chaplain stepped forward and offered up a brief final prayer. Then Captain Wallace asked John if he had any last words. John said, "I'm sorry I killed that man in Savannah. I wasn't sorry at the time, but I've talked to Jesus about it—and I'm sorry now. I ask Jesus and the man's family to forgive me. And I want to thank you all for treating me right while I've been up here." Then he was silent.

One of the guards stepped forward with a small pail of salt water and poured it over the death helmet and the leg wire to ensure good circulating of the electricity. I was disturbed to see the salt water run down across John's face; I was concerned that the salt might be burning his eyes. But John showed no emotion, just sitting still, staring straight ahead.

I saw the chaplain praying softly as a white cloth mask was tied over John's eyes. The guards and the chaplain stepped away from the chair. Behind the chair the executioner and two guards raised their hands to three switches on the big transformers. Two of the switches were disconnected, so that none of the three men knew who was sending a man to his death.

I wanted to close my eyes to the grisly drama, but some powerful force kept my eyes riveted on John Smith. The captain's hand went up—the three black switch handles were pulled down. There was a thudding crunch and loud hum.

I wasn't prepared for what happened next. As the electricity jolted through John's body, he lunged forward, rising and straining against the heavy leather straps in a crouched position. Had he not been tightly bound, he would have landed right in my lap.

For sixty-three seconds his body was submitted to voltage fluctuating between 600 and 1900 volts. When the current was lowered, the body slumped to the seat. Then current was reapplied, and again John's body lunged and strained against the straps. John was dead after the first impact, but the executioner had to go through the procedure three times to be sure. At the second jolt, the salt water on the head and leg began to sizzle.

The electric current was applied a third time and again the body rose against the straps. As curls of smoke rose from the top of John's head, I suddenly smelled the nauseating odor of burning flesh. Sparks flickered in the pool of water on the floor around his right foot. The current was lowered, and one of the guards turned on an overhead exhaust fan to remove the offensive fumes.

The physician gingerly stepped forward, placed a

stethoscope on the chest of the man, and said, "I pronounce this man dead."

I was gripped by another wrenching sight. Although pronounced dead, John was sitting there in the chair slowly nodding his head up and down . . . up and down . . . up and down. A muscle reflex, I supposed. This continued until the guards stepped forward, unbuckled the straps, lifted the body from the chair, and carried it to the morgue.

It was all over. I shut my eyes briefly and silently wept—not for his pain—I'd been assured there was none. Not in sorrow—because he was better off with Jesus. But because of the wasting of a man, God's creation. God never made anybody to be a nobody.

Captain Wallace came over to my chair and quietly said, "Mr. Bradford, I have heard that you are a Christian lawyer—would you like to go in and pray with Callahan while we make preparations for the second execution?"

Numbly, I nodded and stood up, reeling from the lingering shock of what I had seen. The smell of burning human flesh was still in my nostrils.

In the cell block, I found Callahan sitting calmly on his bunk. He must have heard the crunch and hum of the transformers. Yet, when his gray-blue eyes met mine, they were without fear.

His courage lifted my spirits when he said, "I am ready to go and be with Jesus."

Outside the cell, Captain Wallace and his execution

squad started to come for Callahan. Just as the Captain's hand gripped the handle of the iron door to open it—the shrill ring of the telephone on the wall of the execution chamber split the heavy silence.

Those present reacted as though it was a clap of thunder. Every eye was riveted on the telephone as Captain Wallace answered it.

"Yes, Governor," he said into the phone. "No, it's not too late to stop the execution of Callahan. Yes, sir, I will wait for the Pardon and Parole Board's order." With hands that shook, he hung up the telephone.

I was called outside, and Captain Wallace, beaming, said, "I've good news for you, Counselor. The governor just called to tell us that the Parole Board has voted to commute Callahan's death sentence to life. Would you like to tell Callahan?"

"Would I!" My heart leaped within.

I returned to Callahan's cell, trembling with excitement. He looked up—still on his knees, praying.

"Tommy, the good news has come at last. We have won—you are going to live—the governor just called—your sentence is commuted."

Callahan's eyes blurred with tears. "It's Jesus' work, His miracle, isn't it?"

We tried to hug each other through the bars. Then Tommy did a little dance around his cell.

Callahan continued with tears in his eyes, "Brad, I've never met another man like you—you don't know when to quit fighting, do you?"

I just stood there—too choked to say anything more.

When I left Tommy some minutes later he was standing in the middle of his cell, his arms raised and his glowing face lifted up toward the light of the cell's one small window.

As I drove away from the Reidsville Penitentiary, I turned around and looked back at the cold, gray walls of the prison, with its brooding guard towers. The death house atop the institution seemed to glow with a bright light. God's Spirit had surely visited Death Row that day, and brought forth life.

# Epilogue

I had imagined that with the commutation of Callahan's sentence from death to life I would experience a sense of release and could close the Callahan case. But it was not to be—God still had work to do.

One night, several years after Callahan's reprieve from the chair, I was working through the dinner hour alone in my office. Suddenly, I was aware of someone standing in front of my desk. I looked up to see an attractive young woman whom at first I could not place.

"Do you remember me?" she asked. "I'm Mrs. Clyde Tinch."

I remembered the scene in the corridor of the courthouse during Callahan's trial, and it wasn't a pleasant memory. But there was no anger in her face now. Worry lines creased her forehead and her eyes were tearful. I pulled up a chair for her, and suddenly the tears brimmed over.

"I've left my husband," she began. "It's a long

story." She told of the problems they'd had since moving from Atlanta to a city in Alabama. Clyde had gotten a job as a salesman, but soon began to drink heavily.

"My husband hasn't had a good night's sleep since we left Atlanta," she said. "He rolls and tosses and has nightmares. Then he began to accuse me of believing that he was guilty of murdering that grocer. Several weeks ago he threatened to kill me if I didn't stop thinking these thoughts."

She paused to get control of herself. "Last night Clyde came in drunk, and said he had a piece of rope and was going to twist it around my neck and choke me to death when I went to sleep. I stayed up until he passed out. Then I packed our clothes and dressed the children and caught a bus to Atlanta. We're staying at my mother's house. I don't want to divorce Clyde, but I'm afraid to live with him."

"What can I do to help?" I asked, deeply troubled by the anguish of this woman who had believed in her husband.

She asked for prayer and some simple legal advice and departed. I never heard from her again. But her visit changed my thinking toward Clyde Tinch. Now I could feel compassion for him. He was in prison, too—inside himself.

Some years later I learned that he had died of a heart attack. I hope Clyde Tinch squared himself with God before the end.

Billy Joe Tinch was paroled from prison after serving seven years. He became an alcoholic and, like his brother, died of a heart attack not long after his release from prison.

The years passed. Twice Tommy Callahan was turned down when he sought parole. The third time I appeared before the Pardon and Parole Board in his behalf. By now the entire Board had changed. I laid the facts out before them from beginning to end. They took the case under advisement and granted Callahan a parole!

I was about to write him the good news when I remembered that I had an invitation from the chaplain at Reidsville to speak to the inmates the following Sunday. To me this had to be more than coincidence.

On Sunday morning the chaplain met me at the front gate of the prison and escorted me to the chapel. I looked out over the audience of several hundred inmates and spotted Callahan in the fourth row. The Board had delayed notifying him of his parole until I could bring the news in person. That Sunday I opened my Bible to Acts 16:23–40 and told the story of Paul and Silas being cast into prison. At midnight as Paul and Silas prayed and sang praises to God, there was a great earthquake—and immediately all the doors were opened and everyone's bonds were loosed. The Lord had freed Paul and Silas.

At this point in my message, I stopped and called Callahan to come forward. He strode down the aisle, eyes warm in their welcome, and we embraced. With my arm around him, I said, "Now fellows, listen to me—and listen good. Because Callahan and I prayed, God stopped his execution upstairs three times and Tommy didn't have to 'ride the thunderbolt.' Today, because we have continued to pray, God has worked another miracle. The gates of this prison will open, and Tommy Callahan can walk out a free man. He has been granted a pardon. By the authority of the Pardon and Parole Board, Tommy, I bring you this good news."

Tears filled the surprised eyes of Callahan. I heard him whisper, "I'm free—I'm free." The inmates came up out of their chairs, waving and cheering as though they were at a football game.

Callahan had been on parole a couple of years when one night he dropped by his sister's house and met a charming Christian woman. Some time after, she became his wife. A year after his marriage, Callahan received more good news from the Pardon and Parole Board: an order restoring all his civil and political rights.

Today Tommy is an advisor to prison and police officials on crime prevention and prisoner rehabilitation. He is also active in church work, and speaks frequently to civic clubs, prison groups, and schools.

After God's successful completion of the Callahan case, He sent me back to my mother's church, the Wesley Memorial Methodist Church. They asked me to teach a Bible class. Knowing how limited my Scriptural knowledge was, I approached every lesson as a case in court, spending hours in research and preparation. As so often happens, I was, I'm sure, the one who learned the most.

Then one day Jesus placed upon my heart a desire to be God's man on the bench. At the time I was too busy and didn't have the political connections or the money to run for office. So I turned to God in prayer and asked Him to perform a miracle—somehow. Within about twelve months I received a telephone call from the governor of the state of Georgia, offering me a judgeship! The judiciary has become my life's work.

Today, as a Christian judge, I seek daily to dispense justice tempered with mercy to all who come before me, through the wisdom of Jesus Christ.

It is ". . . Not by might, nor by power, but by my spirit, saith the Lord of hosts" (Zechariah 4:6).

*Judge Bradford (left) with T. C. Callahan*